REWIRE

your

BRAIN

Faith-Based Neuroplasticity

Harrison S. Mungal, Ph.D, PsyD

Rewire Your Brain - Faith-Based Neuroplasticity

Unless otherwise identified, Scripture quotations are from

New King James Version of the Bible.

Contact author
www.agetoage.ca
www.harrisonmungal.com
Facebook: Harrison Mungal
Twitter: HarrisonandKathleen @HKrelationships
AgetoAge @agetoagec
LinkedIn: Harrison Mungal, Ph.D., PsyD
YouTube: Harrison Mungal
Phone: 905-533-1334

ABOUT *the* AUTHOR

Harrison Mungal, PhD, PsyD

Dr. Mungal has two doctoral degrees, one in Clinical Psychology and the other in Philosophy in Social Work, dual master's degrees in Social Work and Christian Counselling, and a Bachelor degree in Theology. He worked over 20 years in the fields of mental health and psychiatry then went into psychology. He worked with people from a wide range of backgrounds, including brain injury survivors, refugees, victims of war, PTSD victims, those struggling with mental health and in crisis. He liaison with police, hospitals, community agencies, and inpatient mental health settings.

Dr. Mungal is completely dedicated to improving the lives of his clients. He is known all over the world in over 47 nations for his deep knowledge of neuroscience, mental health, biblical studies and topics supporting individuals, couples and families and businesses.

Dr. Mungal is a highly sought-after workshop presenter who uses his practical approach to help understand the functionality of psychology and spirituality. His global impact is clear from the way he uses humour and enthusiasm to make complicated talks about mental health, addiction, relationships, and parenting at conferences, seminars, and media platforms.

Dr. Mungal's new and scientifically sound methods have been praised by many institutions, earning him awards and recogniztions. He spreads his influence by training and advising a wide range of community partners, such as respected professionals in the fields of medicine, social work, first responders, law enforcement, and senior management teams.

Dr. Mungal is a leader in cutting-edge cognitive research that looks at mental health issues like addiction, psychosis, anxiety, and depression. His work includes research on music therapy and schizophrenia, substance abuse and addictions in the food service industry, and vaccination for children under six years old.

Dr. Mungal practical therapeutic toolbox includes evidence-based therapies including Cognitive Behavioural Therapy (CBT), Cognitive Processing Therapy (CPT), Dialectical Behavioural Therapy (DBT), Thought Developmental Practice (TDP), Acceptance and Commitment Therapy (ACT). Interpersonal therapy (IPT), Motivational Interviewing Techniques, Grounding Techniques, Integrative Eclectic Therapy, Humanistic Experiential Therapy, Interpersonal Therapy, Supportive Therapy, Exposure Therapy, Visual Therapy, Psychodynamic Therapy.

TABLE *Of* CONTENT

INTRODUCTION

In the fast-paced and ever-changing world we live in, it's easy for our minds to get stuck in a web of negative thoughts, self-doubt, and impulsive ideas. We want to stop doing these things and find the strength inside us to improve our lives and make them more enjoyable. In this case, "Rewire Your Brain" is a guiding light that leads to good mental health and a positive way of thinking.

It's even more important to find peace and happiness within yourself in a world that often seems out of control and chaotic. "Rewire Your Brain" is a book that gives you hope and shows you how to make your life better. It offers helpful advice and tips on how to organize your thoughts. This book aims to help you get rid of bad thoughts and feelings and build a healthy mindset through neuroplasticity, mental conditioning, and emotional mastery.

Your brain is always changing. It makes new connections and modifies old ones based on how you think, act, and feel. Neuroplasticity is a fascinating concept that shows how the brain can change and adapt over time. This book discusses it. Learning about neuroplasticity can help you get the most out of your brain. This will change the way your brain works so that you can be stronger, more positive, and grow as a person.

"Rewire Your Brain" is a comprehensive guide that shows you many different ways to take charge of your mind and thoughts. It discusses how to deal with problems and how to be mentally tough so that you can handle anything. You will learn how to free your mind by questioning the thoughts that are keeping you from moving forward. This will help you succeed at work and in your personal life.

This book will help you change the way you talk to yourself so that it matches your biggest goals and lets you control your own mind. You can become a conscious creator by learning how your thoughts affect your health, actions, and feelings. Your life can change if you think positively.

This book is a well-thought-out guide that will help you change the way your brain works. It discusses the interesting idea of neuroplasticity, which shows how amazing the brain is at changing and adapting over time. You can change your brain and overcome the problems that come with negative thought patterns by learning about the principles of neuroplasticity.

"Rewire Your Brain" is based on studies in neuroscience, psychology, and self-improvement. It offers helpful advice on how to get your mind in shape and be mentally stronger. You will learn everything you need to know about how to become mentally tough and resilient. You will learn how to be strong when things get tough. You will learn how to deal with problems with strength and grace, and how to get back on your feet after hard times.

This book will change your life by teaching you how to prevent thoughts that come to you without your control from getting in the way of your progress. It will also teach you how to use the power of positive thinking to help you. The main goal of this journey is to stand up for what you believe in. You will learn how your thoughts can change how you feel, what you do, and how healthy you are. You will learn how to change your thoughts on purpose and with intention by using your mind and the power you have.

"Rewire Your Brain" will teach you how to control your feelings so you can handle problems in a calm and thoughtful way. If you learn how to control your feelings, you won't give in to short-lived urges and patterns of behaviour. Instead, you'll be able to deal with the problems of life with calm and grace. There are also tips in these pages on how to be more positive and make the most of all the good things life has to offer. Having a positive attitude can help you change your life, bring good things into your life, and connect with other people in a real way.

This book discusses how important it is to remember things and create new memories. These memories will help you grow, learn, and change. "Rewire Your Brain" is a comprehensive guide that gives you everything you need to handle the problems of modern life, including tools, information, and motivation. We hope that the journey of a lifetime that you read about on these pages will help you get rid of bad thoughts, accept good ones, and live a life full of meaning, happiness, and contentment. Now is the time to start rewiring!

We haven't used much of the potential that lies deep within our minds. Neuroplasticity, along with our thoughts, feelings, and experiences, can change the very fabric of our lives. "Rewire Your Brain" is an amazing journey of self-discovery and empowerment that shows you how to stay strong and positive for a long time by exploring the mind's complicated pathways.

Negative thoughts can make us feel bad, make it hard to think clearly, and weigh us down. The purpose of this book is to help you deal with these problems, challenge the quick thoughts that keep you from moving forward, and write a new, empowering story about yourself. Learning about the fascinating field of neuroplasticity can help us change who we are. It shows us that the brain can change itself to make us happier and more satisfied.

There are many helpful tips and tools in "Rewire Your Brain" that can help you get your mind ready for success.

Everything changes when we work hard to be positive. "Rewire Your Brain" teaches you a lot about how to think more positively and all the good things that will happen as a result. You can have more happiness, abundance, and peaceful relationships if you change how your brain works to be more positive. This affects more than just your own life.

You need to know how strong your mind is for this journey that will change your life. The Emotional Mind, the Reasonable Mind, and the Wise Mind can help you understand how your thoughts, feelings, and choices all work together. If you can get these parts of your mind to work together, you will become more self-aware, emotionally intelligent, and wise. This will help you be more aware and balanced in your life. Much of our research is about how the Reasonable Mind, the Wise Mind, and the Emotional Mind all work together. These parts of the mind have a lot of power over what we do, what we choose, and what we think. You'll learn a lot about how your mind works by understanding how they work together. This will help you deal with life's problems in a smarter and easier way.

"Rewire Your Brain" also discusses how important it is to remember things and create new memories. We can learn, grow, and change because we can make new memories and keep them. You can change your memories with your brain's power. This will give you a wide range of experiences that will make your life better and help you move on.

This book is a comprehensive guide that includes information from neuroscience, psychology, spirituality and self-help. This approach sees you as a whole person and will help you get your mind back under control and lead it to a better, happier future. When you go on this journey, you start to change. You are in charge of your health, your thoughts, and your feelings.

We hope that these pages will help you change the way you think, get rid of negative thoughts, and use the power of positive thinking to make your life better. May your journey take you to a life that is full of meaning, strength, and happiness that never ends.

Taking care of your brain is an important part of this journey as you learn more about how your mental health affects the choices you make in life. Taking care of yourself, eating well, and exercising regularly can all help your brain work better and make you smarter.

"Rewire Your Brain" knows that real change isn't just about the mind; it's also about giving the brain what it needs to work. We look into how nutrition, exercise, and self-care are all connected and how they can help your brain work better. You can get the most out of your brain by doing things that are good for your health. This will help you focus, make you smarter, and give you a lot of energy.

This book also teaches you how to stay positive so you can get the most out of its great benefits and live a happy and full life. If you change how you think, practice gratitude, and take care of yourself, you will attract experiences that are in line with your highest potential. "Rewire Your Brain" teaches you how to improve yourself, and each step brings you closer to a life full of joy, purpose, and connections with others.

"Rewire Your Brain" also discusses how important it is to make and keep new memories. The brain is like a tapestry of experiences that is always adding to and changing its story. You can unlock your brain's potential for constant growth, deepen your learning, and fill your life with interesting and meaningful moments if you learn how to improve how it makes and keeps memories.

In this book, "Rewire Your Brain" will be your constant guide on this life-changing journey. This book gives you a full plan for getting rid of negative thoughts, stopping beliefs that hold you back, and starting a new time of strength and positivity. It does this by combining new research, old knowledge, and useful exercises. Let's go on a journey of self-discovery together. We'll change the way your brain works so that it can accept all the great things that are possible for you. May this journey give you the strength to create a life full of joy, strength, and deep happiness.

REWIRE *Your* BRAIN

To understand the idea of rewiring the brain, we need to look at how hope and positive thinking can change neuroplasticity. The way we think and feel has a big effect on the brain, changing how it works and how it looks. Positive psychology and building a positive attitude are based on science that can help your brain change and help you grow as a person.

Have you ever felt like you were stuck in a way of thinking or acting that you couldn't change? It could be a habit, a way of thinking, or a reaction that feels like it comes naturally to you. The good news is that it doesn't have to stay that way. Neuroscience has shown us something amazing: our brains can change. Neuroplasticity is the ability to literally change the pathways in our brains that control our thoughts, feelings, and actions.

But long before science found out about neuroplasticity, the Bible was already telling us this. Romans 12:2 says, "Don't follow the pattern of this world; instead, let your mind be renewed." This isn't just flowery language; it's a call from God to change from the inside out.

One of the most complicated and changing systems in the world is the human brain. Scientists thought for a long time that the structure of our brains didn't change much after childhood—that once we became adults, our neural architecture was set in stone. But new discoveries in neuroscience have proven that idea wrong. We now know that the brain is very flexible and can change how it works based on what it learns, what it experiences, and even what hurts it. Neuroplasticity is the name for this process, and it is the basis for how we change the brain.

Neuroplasticity is the brain's ability to make new neural connections and change ones that are already there. These changes can happen at synapses (the places where neurons meet), whole neural circuits, or even between different parts of the brain. The consequences are significant: we can alter our cognition, emotions, and behaviours—not solely on a psychological level, but also biologically.

Motor learning research is one of the best examples of neuroplasticity. Scientists at the University of California San Diego showed in a study published in Nature that learning a new motor skill doesn't just make your brain work harder; it also changes the way the thalamus and motor cortex talk to each other. Researchers used advanced imaging and data analysis to see how practicing the same thing over and over again strengthened some neural connections while shutting down others that weren't related. This selective activation is important for effective learning because it helps the brain wire itself to focus on important signals and block out noise.

This process doesn't just involve motor skills. Neuroplasticity can change how we feel, how we remember things, how we pay attention, and even our personality traits. When we do something or think about it over and over again, we strengthen the neural pathways that go with it.

These pathways take over over time, making the behaviour feel like it happens on its own. On the other hand, a pathway gets weaker and eventually goes away when we stop using it.

This is why habits, whether good or bad, have such a strong effect. They come from neural circuits that have been used a lot. To break a habit, we need to make a new path and make it stronger by doing it over and over. At first, you have to make an effort to do this, but over time it becomes second nature.

This idea is often used in behavioural therapy. For instance, stroke patients who have lost the ability to move a limb are taught to do so again by doing small exercises. Instead of telling patients to move the whole limb at once, therapists tell them to move one finger, then another, slowly rebuilding the neural map for movement. Applied neuroplasticity shows how focused practice can help the brain rewire itself to regain lost functions.

People can rewire their brains to promote resilience and well-being by consistently making healthier choices. Practices like mindfulness, self-reflection, and emotional regulation can change the neural pathways in the brain that are linked to trauma and negative thought patterns.

Another useful tool is visualization. When we mentally practice a behaviour, like speaking with confidence, resisting temptation, or doing a skill, we use the same neural pathways that we would if we were actually doing it. This gets the brain ready to do things in real life and speeds up learning. Athletes, performers, and even people who are recovering from an injury use visualization to improve their performance and speed up their recovery.

Visualization is a strong way to change the way your brain works. Imagining ourselves succeeding, resisting temptation, or walking in peace activates the same neural circuits as actually doing those things. I used this method to help me get over my fear of speaking in front of people. I would close my eyes and picture myself standing tall, speaking clearly, and making a connection with the crowd. I thought about the room, the people, and how calm I felt. My mind started to think it was possible, and it became true.

"Have I not commanded you?" says Joshua 1:9. Be brave and strong. ***"Don't be afraid; don't give up. The Lord your God will be with you wherever you go."*** When we picture things with faith, we put our minds in line with what God has promised.

Changing the way your brain works isn't just about adding new behaviours; it's also about getting rid of old ones. During synaptic pruning, the brain gets rid of connections that aren't being used so that it can make room for more efficient ones. This is why it is important to be consistent. The brain gives more importance to a new behaviour the more we do it. The less we do an old behaviour, the more it goes away.

To change the way our brains work, we need to know how habits are formed. There are three parts to every habit: the cue (or trigger), the routine (the behaviour), and the reward. The cue starts the behaviour, the routine is the action itself, and the reward strengthens the behaviour by releasing dopamine, a chemical that makes you feel good and motivates you.

You want to stop looking at your phone first thing in the morning. The cue is waking up, the routine is getting your phone, and the reward is the dopamine rush you get from notifications. You can change this habit by doing something different, like stretching or writing in a journal, while still getting the reward. Your brain will eventually connect the new behaviour with the same cue and reward, which will change the habit loop.

Environmental cues are very strong. Visual cues, the way things are arranged, and even social situations can all make people act in certain ways. Putting your workout clothes where you can see them can help you get into the habit of working out. Keeping a journal on your nightstand can help you think about what you're thankful for.

Accountability and social support also help us change the way our brains work. When we tell other people about our goals and they encourage us, we turn on reward circuits that make us more motivated. Learning in groups, getting help from a mentor, and getting support from the community all work together to speed up the process of rewiring the brain.

Sleep, food, and exercise are all important parts of rewiring the brain. The brain processes what it has learned and gets rid of metabolic waste while you sleep. Antioxidants, omega-3 fatty acids, and staying hydrated all help keep synapses healthy. Exercise improves blood flow to the brain, boosts growth factors, and enhances cognitive function.

Ultimately, rewiring the brain is a dynamic interplay between intention, repetition, and environment. It's not something that happens once; it's a way of life. The brain is always changing and adjusting. The question is whether we are consciously shaping it or letting it shape itself.

Neuroscience gives us hope. Your brain can change, no matter how old you are, where you come from, or what you've been through. You can learn new things, get rid of bad habits, and develop a growth mindset. The most important things are being consistent, caring, and curious.

When we accept the science that rewires the brain, we enter a new way of changing ourselves. We are not victims of our wiring; we are the ones who make it. And with each deliberate thought, each conscious breath, and each brave decision, we forge new pathways to healing, purpose, and potential.

I remember having anxiety for a long time. I couldn't help but think of the worst possible outcomes. But I started to make new mental paths by praying, writing in a journal, and purposefully replacing negative thoughts. It wasn't right away, but it was real. Philippians 4:8 became my guide: "*Finally, brothers and sisters, whatever is true, whatever is noble, whatever is right, whatever is pure, whatever is lovely, whatever is admirable—if anything is excellent or praiseworthy—think about such things.*"

What we think shapes our reality. The Bible says in Proverbs 23:7, "*For as he thinks in his heart, so is he.*" The things we think about shape who we are. If we keep having negative, fearful, or self-defeating thoughts, those patterns will become ingrained in our brains. But if we choose to think about truth, hope, and grace, we can change the way our minds work to find peace and purpose.

This is why the Bible keeps telling us how important it is to protect our thoughts. 2 Corinthians 10:5 says, "*Take captive every thought and make it obedient to Christ.*" This isn't just a spiritual practice; it's a change in the brain.

Habits are strong because they work without us being aware of them. The brain uses them to save energy. But not all habits are good. Some are bad and keep us stuck in cycles of sin, shame, or not moving forward. We need to find the cue, the routine, and the reward before we can break a habit. If stress makes you eat too much, for instance, the cue is stress, the routine is eating, and the reward is a short time of comfort. To change this habit, you need to replace the routine with a healthier response, such as prayer, exercise, or deep breathing. You still need to find comfort, though.

Galatians 5:16 gives us good advice: "*So I say, walk by the Spirit, and you will not gratify the desires of the flesh.*" We get the strength to make different choices when we let the Holy Spirit into our lives.

Making new habits is like planting seeds. It takes time, effort, and care. Neuroscience shows that doing something over and over again is important. Each time we do a new behaviour, we make the neural pathway that connects it stronger. Begin with little things. Start with five minutes of prayer every day if you want to make it a habit. Set a cue, like lighting a candle or opening your Bible, and then do what you said you would do. Your brain will eventually link that cue with peace and connection.

Psalm 1:2–3 talks about the benefits of regular spiritual practice: "*But his delight is in the law of the Lord, and on his law he meditates day and night.*" He is like a tree that grows by streams of water, bears fruit at the right time, and doesn't lose its leaves. Habits based on God's Word last a long time.

A lot of the ways we think are based on lies, like "I'm not good enough," "I'll never change," and "God doesn't care." These lies become strongholds that shape who we are and how we act.

But the Bible has a lot of truth that can break down these strongholds. Ephesians 4:22–24 says, "*You were taught to put off your old self and be made new in the way you think. You were also taught to put on the new self, which was made to be like God in true righteousness and holiness.*"

The first step is to find the lie. Then find a verse that tells the truth about it. Put it down on paper. Do it every day. Say it out loud. Make it your new mental script.

One of the best ways to rewire your brain is to be thankful. Research shows that being thankful changes the chemistry of the brain, makes you more resilient, and makes you feel better overall. Every day, I write down three things I'm grateful for. Some days it's big, like prayers that are answered or big steps forward. Some days it's little things, like the sun coming through the window or a warm cup of tea. This practice helps me stop thinking about what I don't have and start thinking about what I do have.

"Give thanks in all circumstances; for this is God's will for you in Christ Jesus," says 1 Thessalonians 5:18. Being thankful changes the way our brains work so that we can see God's goodness, even when things are hard.

We weren't meant to change our brains by ourselves. God made us to be part of a community. Hebrews 10:24–25 tells us to *"think about how we can spur each other on to love and good deeds... encouraging each other."* Find someone who will pray with you, check in on you, and celebrate your progress. Tell others about your goals and problems. We become stronger and clearer when we talk about our journey of change.

I used to be part of a small group that worked on spiritual growth. Every week, we talked about what went well and what went wrong. That sense of responsibility helped me stay on track and reminded me that I wasn't alone.

Prayer is more than just talking to God; it's a way to change. When we pray, we connect our minds to heaven. When we think about Scripture, we fill our minds with truth. Psalm 119:15 says, *"I think about your ways and meditate on your rules."* Meditation changes the way we focus. It makes us slower, centers us, and gives us room to grow.

Pick one verse every week and try this. Take your time reading it. Think about every word. Pray that God will talk through it. Let it change the way you think and act.

The process of rewiring the brain isn't straight. There will be times when you fail, fall back, and feel down. But that doesn't mean failure; it means getting better. It says in Proverbs 24:16, *"The righteous fall seven times, but they get back up.*" Every mistake is covered by God's grace. The most important thing is that we keep getting up.

Don't feel bad about yourself when you fall back into an old habit. Think about it, start over, and make a new commitment. You make the new path stronger every time you choose it.

We start to live differently as we change the way our brains work. We respond with kindness instead of anger. We choose to be calm instead of scared. We walk with a purpose instead of being confused.

This change is more than just personal; it's spiritual. "*The mind governed by the flesh is death, but the mind governed by the Spirit is life and peace,*" says Romans 8:6. A brain that has been rewired is a brain that is led by the Spirit. It is a mind that mirrors Christ.

Imagine waking up every day with a clear mind, a happy heart, and the strength to get through anything. Picture yourself dealing with problems with faith instead of fear. That's what happens when you change your mind.

Rewiring the brain is a journey, a process of starting over. It takes time, effort, and grace. But it is possible. And it's worth it. God wants us to change. Not just in how they act, but also in how they think, feel, and see themselves. He gives us new ways to find hope, healing, and holiness.

HARNESSING
NEUROPLASTICITY

I didn't hear the word "neuroplasticity" growing up, but I know it's true. The brain can change, rewire, heal, and grow through experience. When I read the Bible, I see it everywhere—not in scientific terms, but in how God changes minds, hearts, and the way people think.

I have experienced this in my life, particularly during periods of unlearning fear and relearning trust, when grief transformed my internal landscape, and when faith forged new pathways through suffering.

Romans 12:2 says, "***Don't follow the ways of the world; instead, let your mind be renewed***." That verse helped me a lot when I was going back to school, raising seven kids, and trying to get back on my feet after losing someone.

My mind was tired because of all the responsibilities and sadness. But I started to see that renewal didn't happen all at once. It was little choices that made the difference: choosing to be thankful instead of anxious, choosing to pray instead of panic, and choosing to believe that God was still working even when I couldn't see it. Each choice felt like a new groove being carved into my brain, like a spiritual rewiring.

Peter, who said no to Jesus three times. That moment must have burned shame into his mind. But Jesus didn't leave him there. He asked Peter three times after he came back to life, "*Do you love Me?*" (John 21).

It wasn't just forgiving; it was bringing things back together. Jesus was helping Peter rewrite the story, changing failure into love. That's neuroplasticity at work: grace helps memories come back, identities heal, and new emotional pathways form.

I had to do that too. I felt like I was carrying the trauma around with me after my friend Tihomir was killed in Croatia. The loss, the questions, and the feeling of being helpless kept coming back to me. But as time went on, I started to remember things differently through prayer and thinking about them.

I didn't forget the pain, but I began to see the strength, the love, and the legacy. I began to link his memory with purpose rather than despair. It didn't happen all at once; it was the slow work of spiritual neuroplasticity.

Paul says that you should "*take every thought captive to make it obedient to Christ*" (2 Corinthians 10:5). That's not just a metaphor; it's something you do.

I have had to catch thoughts that lead to fear or shame and turn them around to the truth. It's like working out your mind instead of your body. And it gets easier the more I do it.

I've learned that my brain isn't set in stone; it changes. And it starts to change when I fill it with Bible verses, songs of praise, and stories of hope.

This process is even shown in the Psalms. David often begins in despair, asking, "*Why, Lord, do You stand far away?*" (Psalm 10:1)— but it ends with praise. His prayers are like sessions that change how he feels. He talks about his pain, but he doesn't stay there. He chooses to remember how faithful God is and to tell the truth to his soul. "*Bless the Lord, O my soul, and do not forget all His benefits*" (Psalm 103:2). That remembering is very strong. It changes how people feel.

I've noticed this in my writing as well. When I tell stories about people who are strong, when I use Scripture in my writing, I'm not just sharing; I'm healing. I'm reminding myself of things that my mind needs to remember.

I'm making new paths of hope for myself and for other people. Neuroplasticity isn't just a scientific fact; it's a gift from God. The Spirit is what makes life new again.

So I keep making choices. I choose to remember in a different way. I decide to think again. I let God change my mind, one thought at a time.

We can see how Neuroplasticity can help us grow and have a big impact on our mental health. Neuroplasticity is the brain's amazing ability to change and grow by making new neural connections and changing old ones all the time. It is a simple process that helps us learn, grow, and change.

We should look into the different ways that science has shown can change how our brains work. This will help us change the way our brains work so that we can get better.

We can see how much it could change our lives and minds if we understand its main ideas. We need to learn more about how the brain can change and how it does so all the time based on what we do, think, and feel.

Neuroplasticity is the brain's amazing ability to change, adapt, and reorganize itself when it learns new things or has new experiences. It means that the brain can make new neural connections, make old ones stronger, and even move functions to other parts of the brain. This idea goes against the long-held belief that the brain is a stable and unchanging organ.

Neuroplasticity exhibits two principal forms: structural and functional alterations. Structural changes are all about how the connections between neurons change. This could mean making new neurons, new synapses (connections between neurons), or changing how connections that are already there work. Functional changes that include changes to the strength and effectiveness of existing neural pathways.

Neuroplasticity happens in many ways, such as synaptic plasticity, neurogenesis, and cortical remapping. Synaptic plasticity is the ability of synapses to change strength based on how active and how often neurons are.

Neurogenesis is the process of making new neurons. It mostly happens in certain areas of the brain, like the hippocampus. Cortical remapping is when the brain changes how it maps out its movements and senses. For instance, when the visual cortex of a blind person starts to respond to touch.

Experiences and the environment have a big effect on neuroplasticity. The brain changes based on what we do, learn, and think about. This is what scientists call "experience-dependent plasticity." Learning to play an instrument, for example, can change how the brain's motor and auditory areas work, which can help you get better at music.

Neuroplasticity is very important for brain development in the early stages because it helps the brain adapt to its surroundings and make important neural circuits. Plasticity, on the other hand, lasts for life, but not as long. It helps people learn new things, get better after getting hurt, and get used to changes in their surroundings. People with neurological disorders can find hope in lifelong plasticity because it shows that the brain can move functions to healthier areas to make up for areas that are damaged.

Learning about neuroplasticity is important for how people grow and get better. This means that our brains aren't set in stone; they can change and grow. Neuroplasticity lets us change how our brains work so we can learn new skills, make new habits, deal with problems, and feel better mentally. The next parts of this book will talk about different ways you can use neuroplasticity to help you become a better person.

Neuroplasticity is a fundamental concept that contradicts the notion of a static brain. It shows that the brain can change how it works depending on what it learns, what it goes through, and where it is. When you want to know more about how neuroplasticity can help you grow and change as a person, the first thing you should do is learn the basics.

As we get older, it's even more important to keep our brains and minds sharp. We need to learn more about how the brain ages and how to keep our cognitive skills sharp as we get older and promote neuroplasticity.

We can learn how to make the most of the brain's amazing ability to change by learning about neuroplasticity and how to use it in different ways. By comprehending and utilizing neuroplasticity, we embark on a transformative journey of personal development and realize our complete potential.

There is also a connection between neuroplasticity and learning. You can remember what you've learned, learn new skills, and improve your memory by using strategies and techniques. We can make the brain more flexible so that we can learn more. We can use spaced repetition and practice on purpose, for example.

Creativity, an essential component of human expression, is closely linked to neuroplasticity. We ought to investigate how the brain's capacity for self-modification can enhance our creativity. We can think of new things and be creative if we learn how the brain works.

Neuroscience has taught us a lot about neuroplasticity, which is the brain's amazing ability to change and adapt over time. This ability to change also affects how we learn and remember things, which gives us useful information about how to improve our memory and thinking. Learning about neuroplasticity can help us find better ways to learn and get the most out of our mental efforts.

A key part of learning through neuroplasticity is knowing how important it is to be involved and take part. We can only learn so much by just reading or listening to things. Active recall and elaboration are two ways to interact with the material that can only help memory formation.

Active recall means getting information from our memory instead of just looking it over. This exercise makes our brains work harder to strengthen the neural connections that are linked to that information, which makes it easier to remember later. We've heard that flashcards, quizzes, and writing down important ideas in our own words can help us remember things and make the brain pathways that help us store and get information stronger. This might be true in some ways.

On the other hand, elaboration means adding to what we already know and connecting new information to what we already know. We can make a rich web of connections when we link new ideas to things we already know. This helps us remember and use new information more easily. This method helps the brain make new synaptic connections and makes the neural circuits that are linked to what you've learned stronger.

Another good way to use neuroplasticity to help us learn is to say things again and again. You should review what you've learned over time instead of cramming it all into one session. This will help your long-term memory. This method works because seeing things over and over again makes our brains remember them better. When we space out the time between review sessions, memory reconsolidation happens. This makes the memory traces stronger and more stable, which makes the information last longer and easier to find.

Adding experiences that use more than one sense can also help our brains change. When you use more than one sense, like sight, sound, touch, and even movement, different parts of your brain work together and make connections stronger. Learning can be more fun and help different neural networks that are related to what was learned when you use pictures, sounds, and hands-on activities or interactive simulations.

Neuroplasticity encompasses cognitive functions, including memory and learning, as well as the domain of creativity. The brain is a great place to encourage creative thinking because it can change and adapt to new things and experiences.

Neuroplasticity alters cognitive processes, potentially influencing creativity. Divergent thinking is the ability to come up with many different ways to answer a question or solve a problem. Neuroplasticity improves divergent thinking by making it easier for different parts of the brain to connect and for new neural pathways to form. This increased connectivity makes it easier to combine ideas and information from different areas, which leads to new and creative solutions.

Neuroplasticity also helps people be creative by letting them use different parts of their brains. Flexible thinkers are people who can change how they see things, get out of their usual ways of thinking, and look at problems from different points of view.

Neuroplasticity allows our brains to rewire themselves, which helps people learn new ways of thinking and get out of their old ways of thinking. Creative insights come from being open to new ideas and being able to connect different ones.

Doing things that make neuroplasticity work can help us be more creative. Art, like painting, drawing, or playing an instrument, can make different parts of our brains work harder and help new neural connections form. You can also improve neuroplasticity by doing things like brainstorming, solving problems, and doing creative exercises. These things make our brains work in new ways and see new choices.

Keep in mind that being creative isn't just about making art. It affects many parts of life, such as how technology improves, how science finds new things, and how to solve everyday problems. So, encouraging creativity through neuroplasticity can have a big impact on your health, career, and personal growth.

The link between creativity and neuroplasticity shows how well our brains can change and adapt, which helps us think of new ways to solve problems. We can use neuroplasticity to unlock our creative potential, become more open-minded, and look at problems in new ways. Doing things that help neuroplasticity can make you more creative and help you grow as a person. This can help you think of new things and make your life happier and more complete.

A lot of us are very worried about keeping our brains sharp and our cognitive function as we get older. Neuroplasticity does give us some hope in this area, though. Neuroplasticity is still a strong force in our lives as we get older. We can improve our cognitive skills and keep our minds sharp as we get older by learning how to use neuroplasticity.

Doing cognitive training exercises is one way to help neuroplasticity as people get older. These tasks test our memory, focus, and ability to solve problems by making us do different things. Doing these exercises often can get your brain working, which makes it change and rewire itself. This can help you stay sharp and make your thoughts clearer.

Memory and learning are also very closely linked to neuroplasticity. We have used good learning methods to take advantage of the brain's ability to change and learn new things. By practicing, repeating, and being involved, we have used neuroplasticity to make it easier for us to learn and grow our minds.

Neuroplasticity is a key factor in developing emotional intelligence, an essential skill for navigating life's challenges. We should learn how to make our emotional intelligence better and grow by doing things that make our brains more flexible. Being more self-aware, empathetic, and in control of our emotions can make us stronger and happier in both our personal and professional lives.

Neuroplasticity has a big impact on emotional intelligence, which is important for our health and relationships. Emotional intelligence means being able to handle your own feelings and being able to understand and care about how other people feel. Learning how neuroplasticity can make us more emotionally intelligent can help us become stronger, better at dealing with problems, and better at handling our emotions.

We can change and adapt our brains throughout our lives, which gives us hope that we can build and strengthen the neural pathways that are linked to emotional intelligence. We can change how our brains work to make us more emotionally aware, empathetic, and strong if we work hard.

Neuroplasticity can also help people become more emotionally intelligent by making their environment more positive and supportive.

Being around people who make us happy and inspire us can make our bodies make oxytocin, a hormone that is linked to happiness and trust. We can make our brains work better for emotional intelligence by making meaningful connections and building healthy relationships.

One way to use neuroplasticity to improve your emotional intelligence is to work on having a good attitude and feeling good about things. Joy, gratitude, and love are all good feelings that can change how neurons connect and make you feel better emotionally. We can make the neural connections that are linked to emotional intelligence stronger by consciously thinking about good things and having a positive attitude.

To be emotionally intelligent, you need to learn how to be aware of yourself and how other people feel. We can strengthen the neural pathways that are linked to emotional intelligence by thinking about ourselves and trying to understand how other people feel and see things. This can help you get to know other people better, talk to them better, and get along with them better.

Neuroplasticity is the brain's ability to change the way it works, and being positive and hopeful can have a big effect on it. Studies indicate that fostering a positive mindset can improve brain plasticity, resulting in various advantages for personal growth and health.

When you question and change negative thought patterns, the brain's neuroplasticity mechanisms are turned on. When we question our automatic thoughts on a regular basis, new neural connections form that let us mix in thoughts and beliefs that are healthier and more flexible. This rewiring of the brain can improve your emotional health and behaviour a lot over time.

Neuroplasticity is still a great way to keep our brains sharp and our minds busy as we get older. We can keep our brains flexible and help them age well by doing cognitive training exercises, getting regular exercise, making friends, eating a healthy diet, and managing stress. You can keep your mind sharp and live a full and interesting life as you get older if you stay active.

Let's celebrate how neuroplasticity can change things as we finish this chapter on rewiring the brain. Our brains are really good at changing, adapting, and growing. This chapter has given us the tools we need to reach our full potential and start a journey of personal growth, resilience, and lifelong learning. We can all make things better by changing our brains. Every step we take with a goal makes the future better and more enjoyable.

POSITIVE THINKING

Thinking positively also makes you stronger and helps you learn how to deal with problems in a healthy way. People who are optimistic usually believe that problems or setbacks are only temporary and not permanent or widespread. They can bounce back from hard times more easily because they think they can find solutions to their problems. We can help people be more flexible and adaptable when things get tough by helping them build resilience.

Thinking positively can also help people change their beliefs and the way they think. We can change how our brains work by questioning negative beliefs and having a positive attitude. This cognitive restructuring helps people grow and find new chances by making new connections in their brains.

Being positive and hopeful can have a big impact on neuroplasticity and how you grow as a person. We can become more resilient, less stressed, more creative, and more flexible by changing the way we think. One of the best ways to use neuroplasticity to improve yourself and your life is to be positive.

Also, being positive has been linked to less stress and worry. Stress for a long time can stop neuroplasticity, which is bad for your mental and emotional health. A good attitude can help us handle stress and keep our brains safe from the bad effects of stress over time. This, in turn, makes the environment good for neuroplasticity and personal growth.

When we think positively, our brains make and strengthen neural pathways that are connected to good thoughts and feelings. This process makes the brain think positively in the future, which makes the cycle stronger. These neural pathways work better when you keep thinking positively, which makes it easier for you to do so.

Being positive makes you more open-minded and adaptable, which are both important for coming up with new ideas and finding solutions to problems. We can come up with new ways to solve problems and see them from different angles when we have a good attitude. This mental flexibility helps new neural connections form, which makes you think of more creative things.

For example, "***This is the day the Lord has made; I will rejoice and be glad in it***" (Psalm 118:24). That isn't just a verse to me; it's a choice. I am choosing to think positively, not because everything is easy, but because God is still with me.

Philippians 4:8 is a key verse for me: "***Think about things that are true, noble, right, pure, lovely, and admirable.***" That's how I think about things. I said, "Is this true?" when I was scared. I asked, "Is this lovely?" when shame whispered. That verse helped me change the way I think, and over time, I saw a change in my mood and my spirit.

This kind of thinking is all over Paul's letters. He writes from prison, "***Always be happy in the Lord.***" I will say it again: Be happy!

(Philippians 4:4) That kind of happiness doesn't depend on what's going on around you; it's spiritual.

I've learned to be happy about little things, like a peaceful moment, a kind word, or a big step forward in my writing. Each one is a sign that God is still at work.

Jesus even talked about joy when he was about to die. "*For the joy set before Him, He endured the cross,"* says Hebrews 12:2. That verse makes me think that being positive isn't silly; it's prophetic. It looks past the pain to the promise.

I had to do that on my own journey—when I was up late at night editing chapters, when I was helping others through their own storms, and when I chose to believe that my story still matters.

For me, positive thinking is a spiritual practice. It's choosing to tell the truth, remember grace, and hope for good things. It's not about pretending everything is fine; it's about having faith that God is. And every time I choose that position, I feel my mind clear, my heart lift, and my spirit come into line with the One who makes everything new.

Mindfulness and meditation are part of positive thinking which have become very popular in the last few years because they have been good for your health and your brain's ability to change. These practices entail fostering a condition of concentrated attention and awareness of the present moment, devoid of judgment or attachment to thoughts or emotions. Mindfulness and meditation can help the brain rewire itself, which can change how neurons work and how they are built in a number of good ways.

Long-term stress can make neuroplasticity worse and hurt your mental and physical health in a lot of ways. Mindfulness and meditation can help neuroplasticity grow by making stress less of a problem over time. Mindfulness and meditation are two great ways to help people grow and make their brains more flexible.

Changing how the brain works, making it less likely to wander, boosting cognitive functions, and making you feel better emotionally are all ways that these activities can help the brain rewire itself in good ways.

Meditation and mindfulness can help you learn more about yourself, get stronger, and make your mind more flexible and open. Both concepts have been shown to affect the prefrontal cortex, which is in charge of making decisions, controlling emotions, and higher-level thinking. These changes to the structure suggest that cognitive functions, emotional health, self-awareness, and impulse control have all gotten better.

Mindfulness and meditation also help people notice and accept what's going on right now, like thoughts, feelings, and sensations, without judging them. By not reacting, we can see what's going on inside us without getting involved. This skill can help us better control our thoughts and feelings, which is good for neuroplasticity.

A lot of people are talking about mindfulness and meditation these days. These are great ways to boost neuroplasticity. We can change the way our brains work and how they are built by training them to be present and developing a state of focused awareness. This can help our emotional health, resilience, and cognitive abilities.

You need to deal with stress and put your mental health first if you want to keep your brain healthy. Long-term stress can hurt neuroplasticity and cognitive skills. So, doing things that help you relax, like yoga, tai chi, mindfulness meditation, or deep breathing exercises, can help your brain stay flexible and lessen the bad effects of stress.

HEALTHY LIFESTYLE

It's important to live a healthy lifestyle to keep your brain and mind sharp. As we get older, a lot of things we do every day can hurt our brains. For instance, regular exercise has been shown to improve neuroplasticity and stop cognitive function from getting worse.

Living a healthy life is no longer just a personal goal; it's a spiritual practice that honours the life God gave me. I didn't always think that way. For years, I was so focused on surviving—but as time went on, I started to see that not taking care of my body was hurting everything: my relationships, my energy, my clarity, and even my ability to hear God clearly. It didn't happen all at once, but the Bible started to speak to me in new ways.

One verse that really hit home for me was 1 Corinthians 6:19–20: ***"Do you not know that your bodies are temples of the Holy Spirit..."*** You are not your own; someone paid for you.

So, with your bodies, honour God. That verse made me stop. I always thought of my body as a tool that helped me get through the day. But this verse changed it into a holy place. If my body is a temple, then how I treat it is important for both me and the Spirit that lives inside of me.

I began to make little changes. I started walking every day, not just to get some exercise, but also to pray and clear my mind. I picked foods that fed me instead of numbing me. I put sleep first, even if it meant turning down late-night work. And I saw something: I was more present. More patient. Happier. My kids felt it. My wife felt it. My writing even felt it. It wasn't just about me feeling better; it was also about me being better for other people.

"Above all else, guard your heart, for everything you do flows from it," says Proverbs 4:23. That includes being healthy physically.

When I'm tired and worn out, I'm more likely to react, feel anxious, and feel like I'm not connected to others. But when I am well-rested and well-fed, I can protect my heart with wisdom. I can respond with grace. I can love for a long time. A healthy lifestyle gives you emotional and spiritual space.

This is a great example set by Jesus. He went to quiet places to pray and rest (Luke 5:16). He never rushed and ate and walked with purpose. His life was busy, but not too busy. That makes me think. I've learned that taking a break isn't being lazy; it's following orders. That taking care of my body is not being vain; it's being responsible. That movement isn't punishment; it's a celebration.

I've also seen how my decisions affect other people. My kids learn to care about their bodies when I make meals with care. They see that peace is possible when I take the time to stretch or breathe deeply. They learn that boundaries are sacred when I say no to too many commitments. My way of life becomes a living testimony—not of perfection, but of grace in action.

The Bible says in Romans 12:1, "*Offer your bodies as a living sacrifice, holy and pleasing to God—this is your true and proper worship.*" That verse makes me think that being healthy is a form of worship.

Every bite, breath, and step can be a gift. People are drawn to wellness when I live that way, but they are also drawn to the One who makes it meaningful.

I've seen the difference even in my work as a psychologist and a minister. When I get enough sleep and my mind is clear, I can listen better, speak more clearly, and serve with more joy. Being there for someone becomes a gift, not a burden. My energy is a gift, not a burden. That's the magic of living a healthy life: it makes love grow.

So I keep picking health. Not to chase after an image, but to show a calling. I take care of my body so I can take care of other people. I sleep so I can get up. I feed myself so I can take care of others. And through it all, I remember that this life is a gift and that I want to live it well— for God, for my family, and for everyone I am meant to touch.

Exercise makes blood flow to the brain better, releases good neurochemicals, and helps new neurons and synaptic connections grow. Walking, swimming, and dancing are all good for our brains and our ability to think.

Exercise is good for our health in many ways, and it also makes our brains work better. Exercise gets a lot of things in the body moving, which can be good for the brain. Our hearts beat faster and blood flows better to our brains when we work out. This gives our brains the oxygen and other nutrients they need. This extra blood flow helps new blood vessels grow and releases growth factors that help new neurons and synapses grow.

Exercise makes neurotrophic factors, which are proteins that help neurons stay alive and grow. They also help synaptic connections form and get stronger. This is one of the most important ways that exercise helps the brain change and grow. Exercise is good for our mental health and mood because it makes our brains work better and look better. This has an indirect effect on neuroplasticity.

Endorphins are chemicals in the brain that make you feel good. When you work out, these chemicals are let out. Working out regularly can help with anxiety, depression, and stress. All of these things can make your brain a better place for neuroplasticity to grow.

Keep in mind that different kinds of exercise can change the brain in different ways. Running, swimming, and other aerobic activities, as well as weightlifting, yoga, and other resistance training, can help the brain change its structure. We can also benefit in other ways by changing up our workouts. Your brain has to work harder to learn new ways to move and motor skills when you try new things. This is good for neuroplasticity.

It turns out that exercise is also a great way to change how the brain works. Movement and neuroplasticity is the study of how different types of exercise can help your brain work better, remember things better, and improve your overall cognitive health. We learn that different kinds of exercise, like aerobics, strength training, and even just moving around every day, can change the brain.

Exercising is a great way to use neuroplasticity and help yourself grow in many ways. Regular exercise can improve our mental health, help us think more clearly, and make us feel better emotionally. You can add physical activity to your daily routine to help your brain adapt and rewire itself. For example, you could go for a brisk walk, take a yoga class, or play tennis.

Food is very important for your brain's health, so you can't ignore it. We look at how diet affects neuroplasticity, focusing on how certain nutrients and ways of eating can help the brain work better and encourage neuroplastic changes. We need to learn more about how inflammation, gut health, and brain health are all connected. This will help us learn more about how the foods we eat can change how well we think.

The brain needs the right kinds of food to work right. It affects memory, the ability to think, and the brain's ability to change itself. A healthy and balanced diet can help our own growth and health as well as neuroplasticity.

Nutrition for neuroplasticity includes getting enough of the nutrients your body needs. These are vitamins, minerals, omega-3 fatty acids, and antioxidants that keep the brain healthy and help it work. Omega-3 fatty acids are good for brain cells because they help them grow and stay healthy. Salmon and walnuts are two foods that have a lot of omega-3 fatty acids. These good fats also help lower inflammation in the brain, which can make it harder for neuroplasticity to happen.

Antioxidants are very important for protecting the brain from oxidative stress, and fruits and vegetables are full of them. Free radicals can hurt brain cells and make it harder for the brain to change and adapt when they build up. Eating a lot of colorful fruits and vegetables, like berries, spinach, and broccoli, can give your brain a lot of antioxidants.

For neuroplasticity to work, it also needs vitamins and minerals. B vitamins, especially B6, B9 (folate), and B12, are important for making neurotransmitters. These are very important for brain cells to communicate with each other.

Many foods, such as leafy greens, legumes, and fortified cereals, contain B vitamins. Iron, zinc, and magnesium are other minerals that are very important for how our brains work and how they change over time. You can keep your brain healthy by eating foods that are high in iron, like spinach and lean meats; foods that are high in zinc, like oysters and pumpkin seeds; and foods that are high in magnesium, like dark chocolate and avocados.

It's important to remember that a healthy diet for our brains isn't just about getting enough of some vitamins and minerals. A healthy and varied diet is important because it gives the brain everything it needs to work well. When you eat a lot of whole foods, like lean proteins, whole grains, fruits, vegetables, and healthy fats, your brain gets all the nutrients it needs.

Eating a lot of processed foods, saturated fats, refined sugars, and alcohol, on the other hand, can make cognitive decline worse and neuroplasticity less effective. Diets like this can cause inflammation, oxidative stress, and an imbalance in neurotransmitters, which can all make it harder for the brain to change and adapt.

Eating a balanced diet with lots of fruits and vegetables and cutting back on processed foods and bad fats can also help your brain stay healthy and make it easier for you to learn, grow, and get over setbacks.

We shouldn't forget how important sleep is for learning and neuroplasticity. Our brains work on and combine new information while we sleep. This helps us remember things better and makes us smarter overall. Getting enough good sleep is very important for neuroplasticity and making learning easier. Making the bedroom a good place to sleep and sticking to a regular sleep schedule are two good sleep habits that can really help with memory consolidation and retention.

Creativity is a big part of what makes people smart, and people have praised it for being able to come up with new ideas and inventions throughout history. When we think in new and creative ways, we can find new ways to solve problems and link ideas that don't seem to fit together.

Older adults who stay in touch with friends and family and hang out with other people tend to have better brain function. Being with other people is good for your mental health, helps you deal with your emotions, and gives you chances to learn and think critically. Your brain can change and your overall cognitive health can get better if you join social groups, volunteer, or do hobbies that require you to talk to other people.

Lastly, we know that neuroplasticity is very important for keeping our minds and brains sharp as we get older. By accepting the ideas behind neuroplasticity, we have given ourselves the power to keep our minds sharp and fight the cognitive decline that comes with age. Taking care of our brains and knowing that we can live a full and happy life at any age by learning new things, doing brain exercises, and taking a whole-person approach to brain health.

NEUROSCIENCE OF HABITS

At one moment or another, you probably gathered your courage and made a solemn vow to improve your life. Maybe you promised to eat healthier, exercise more, pray daily, or finally break that one habit that's been holding you back. You felt hopeful, determined—even excited. But then, three months later, you slowly realized you had failed miserably to keep your promise. Guilt started dancing a paso doble with discouragement, and deep down, you felt oddly relieved. You didn't have to fake it anymore. You could drop the effort and return to your old ways.

Sound familiar? If so, you're not alone. That just makes you a normal human being with some real-life experience. I've been there too—more times than I'd like to admit. So why is it so hard to keep resolutions or follow through with personal change?

It has everything to do with how our brains are wired. Neuroscience shows us that the information in our brain follows certain paths. The more we use a path, the stronger it becomes. It's like building a superhighway—information travels faster and easier along it. But if we want to take a different path, we have to consciously override the autopilot, and that demands serious mental effort.

This is exactly what happens when we try to form new habits. At first, the old highway is still dominant. The new path is just a dirt trail. So our brain naturally defaults to the old route. Only by consistently choosing the new path—again and again—can we begin to shift the balance. Over time, the old road shrinks, and the new one expands.

But here's the tricky part: motivation. Specifically, the difference between intrinsic and extrinsic motivation. When we make changes based on intrinsic motivation—things that truly matter to us personally—it becomes easier to override the autopilot. The joy and satisfaction we get from the new habit itself help us stick with it.

The problem is most of our attempts to change are tied to extrinsic motivators. We reward ourselves for effort with treats, praise, or results. But extrinsic motivators are not sustainable. They're result-driven. If we don't see results, we lose the reward—and the motivation disappears. That's why so many new habits fail.

I remember trying to wake up early to pray and read Scripture. I told myself I'd reward the effort with coffee and a pastry from my favorite café. But if I overslept or missed a day, I felt doubly punished—no prayer and no treat.

Eventually, I gave up. It wasn't until I started linking my morning quiet time to something I genuinely loved—watching the sunrise and journaling my prayers—that it became sustainable.

Psalm 5:3 says, *"In the morning, Lord, you hear my voice; in the morning I lay my requests before you and wait expectantly."* That verse became my anchor.

Let me give you another example. Imagine a student who wants to lose weight. She goes to the gym, which she hates, and rewards herself with shopping every time she loses a pound. That's an extrinsic motivator. If she doesn't lose weight, there's no reward—and quitting is just around the corner.

Instead, she should link the activity—exercising—to something she genuinely enjoys. If she's social, she could go to the gym with friends. If she loves music, she could work out while listening to her favourite band. If she's competitive, she could challenge herself with goals or apps. This way, the activity itself becomes rewarding, not just the result.

Even if she doesn't lose weight one week, she's not punishing herself. She's still enjoying the process. That's the power of intrinsic motivation. It makes habits enjoyable—and sustainable.

So what should we do if we want to change a habit or develop a new one?

First, make a list of things you're naturally drawn to—things that bring you joy and give you energy. Second, link one or more of those things to the new habit you want to build. When I say "link," I mean do them at the same time. That's it.

Your brain will begin to associate the new habit with the pleasure of the activity you enjoy. It's all about that little dopamine rush we get when we're doing something we love. Proverbs 17:22 says, *"A cheerful heart is good medicine, but a crushed spirit dries up the bones."* Joy is not just emotional—it's neurological.

So if you're a social person, link your new habit to spending time with friends. If you love music, do your habit while listening to your favorite band. If you love nature, take your habit outdoors. Just experiment and see what works best for you.

And remember: God designed our brains to grow, adapt, and renew. Romans 12:2 reminds us, ***"Do not conform to the pattern of this world, but be transformed by the renewing of your mind."*** That transformation is possible—one habit, one step, one joyful moment at a time.

As we age, something interesting happens in our brains. The neural pathways we've built over time—the ones we've reinforced through repetition—become stronger and more dominant. In other words, we become more of ourselves. That's not necessarily a bad thing, but it does mean that change becomes harder. Adapting to new things takes more effort.

I've seen this firsthand. I remember watching my mom try to use her new cell phone. She tapped the screen like it might bite her. Meanwhile, my granddaughter, just six years old, figured it out in minutes through trial and error. It made me wonder: are older people just less capable of adapting? Of course not. They absolutely can adapt—it just takes longer and requires more intentional effort.

One theory behind this growing rigidity is that we stop learning new things. I'm not talking about casual learning—I mean deep, focused, immersive learning. The kind that stretches us. When we stop using the brain's plasticity, we begin to lose it. It's like a muscle: use it or lose it.

Middle age is a critical time. Life feels stable, we've mastered our routines, and we often stop challenging ourselves. We replay the same skills over and over, but that's not learning. That's repetition. And repetition doesn't create structural change in the brain. Before we know it, the last time we truly learned something new was decades ago.

So what can we do? What should we do?

The answer is simple: learn something new. Really learn it. Dive in with focus and commitment. Proverbs 1:5 says, "***Let the wise listen and add to their learning, and let the discerning get guidance***." Learning isn't just for the young—it's for the wise.

We need to explore exercises to build mental flexibility. They are great starting points, but we need to go deeper. Exercises require repetition, commitment, and a willingness to stretch. They're designed to stimulate your brain and lead to lasting structural changes.

I recently started playing the piano. At first, my fingers felt like strangers to the keys. But week after week, I noticed progress. My hands moved more fluidly, and I could feel my brain adapting.

It's the closest I've come to watching my brain grow. Psalm 33:3 says, "***Sing to him a new song; play skillfully, and shout for joy***." There's joy in learning something new—even when it's hard.

Typing with all ten fingers is another powerful exercise I try to apply on my laptop. If you already do, try switching hands on the keyboard. It's awkward, yes, but it gives your brain a real workout. I tried this once and laughed at how slow I was—but I also felt alive, challenged, and engaged.

Gardening is another beautiful way to engage your senses. Its one of my favourite I look forward to every summer. Whether it's a rooftop flower box or a backyard vegetable box, gardening connects you to the earth. I remember planting tomatoes and hot peppers one summer. The smell of the soil, the feel of the leaves, the joy of harvesting—it was healing. Genesis 2:15 reminds us that God placed man in the garden "***to work it and take care of it***." There's something sacred about tending to life.

Volunteering is one of the most transformative things I've ever done. I've worked at a prison with young offenders, with street children in Toronto with our children when they were younger, homeless communities, and even refugees in Croatia during the war with Serbia. Each experience stretched me. Volunteering in a prison, changed how I see humanity. Proverbs 11:25 says, *"A generous person will prosper; whoever refreshes others will be refreshed."* When we serve, we grow.

Joining a local gym was one of the most unexpected joys of my life. I wasn't motivated to go, did not feel I have the body type—I went and felt I was just in the background of those who are experienced—but meeting a guy name Daniel who was trained and experienced in working out, shifted my perspective. It wasn't about going to the gym any longer; it was about stepping out of my comfort zone. It reminded me of 2 Timothy 1:7: *"For God gave us a spirit not of fear but of power and love and self-control."* Trying something new builds courage.

Lifelong learning is more than a trend—it's a necessity. Whether it's diving deeper into your profession or exploring a passion, studying keeps your mind sharp. I once took a course on Mental Health and AI just because I was curious. It opened my eyes to the advancement of our world. Ecclesiastes 7:12 says, *"Wisdom preserves those who have it."* Keep learning.

Learning a new language is phenomenal for your brain. I've always loved the sound of Spanish, German and French, so I started learning it. It's tough but thrilling. Even sign language or Braille can open new neural pathways. It's like giving your brain a new set of tools to explore the world. Psalm 19:3 says, *"There is no speech or language where their voice is not heard."* Every language carries beauty and meaning.

Keeping a diary might seem simple, but it's deeply powerful. I started journaling again recently. Just a few lines each night—what I felt, what I learned, what I'm grateful for. It helps me hear my own heart more clearly. Lamentations 3:40 says, *"Let us examine our ways and test them, and let us return to the Lord."* Reflection is a path to renewal.

These are some lasting connections in your brain which will give your mind a meaningful workout. These practices aren't just about mental health. They're about spiritual growth, emotional resilience, and staying connected to the world and to God.

In the coming sessions, we'll explore how habits are formed and how we can reshape them. But for now, I invite you to pick one of these exercises and begin. Let's renew our minds together. Let's stay curious, compassionate, and courageous. And above all, let's trust that God is still shaping us—no matter our age.

Romans 12:2 says it best: *"Do not conform to the pattern of this world, but be transformed by the renewing of your mind."* Let's live that transformation—one step, one stretch, one new beginning at a time.

CHANGING Existing
HABITS

Habits emerge because our brains are constantly on the lookout for ways to save effort. You could call it laziness, but I prefer to think of it as energy efficiency. Without habits, our brains would be overwhelmed by the constant input and decisions we face daily. We'd shut down, mentally paralyzed by the sheer volume of choices.

When a habit forms, the brain stops fully participating in decision-making. That means unless we deliberately and consciously go against the habit, the action will take place automatically. And here's something fascinating: habits never truly disappear. At best, they become dormant and lose some of their sharpness over time—but they're still there.

It's like swimming or riding a bike. Once it's in our system, it stays. Every winter, I'm amazed at how easily I pick up ice skating again, even though I haven't done it for a while. That's the beauty of habit—it's efficient. Imagine having to relearn driving every time you return from vacation. That wouldn't do.

But here's the issue: our brains can't tell the difference between a good habit and a bad one. From a neurological perspective, it's just an action that needs to be performed as efficiently as possible. There's no moral judgment involved. This leads us to develop bad habits—ones that don't serve us and can even harm our health, relationships, or spiritual life.

These bad habits, like the good ones, don't simply vanish. Even when we disavow them, they lie dormant, ready to be activated—especially under stress or temptation. Proverbs 25:28 says, *"**Like a city whose walls are broken through is a person who lacks self-control.**"*

Habits are powerful. They can emerge outside our awareness or be deliberately designed. The good news is, they can also be reshaped once we understand how they work.

A habit is essentially an association of three parts: the cue (or trigger), the routine (the action itself), and the reward. The cue is what activates the habit—the signal your brain picks up to initiate the automated behaviour. For example, waking up is a cue. What do you do next? Hit snooze? Get out of bed? Say good morning to your spouse? Chances are, you're not even thinking about it anymore—it's automatic.

The routine can be physical, mental, or emotional. A song might make you feel nostalgic. A place might remind you of someone. Witnessing conflict might stir anger or sadness. The habit forms when the routine is followed by a reward—a signal to your brain that this association is worth remembering. Rewards can be anything from food or caffeine to emotional payoffs like praise or self-congratulation. On a chemical level, it's all about dopamine—that little rush we get when we enjoy something.

Over time, if repeated enough, these associations—cue, routine, and reward—become intertwined. And dopamine doesn't just respond to the reward; it also fuels anticipation and craving. So when the cue appears, we feel a strong urge to perform the routine and receive the reward.

So how do we change a habit?

First, we must become aware of our habits and identify the three parts. Once we understand how the habit works, we can tweak or replace any part of it. The trigger is usually the starting point. From there, we crave the reward and perform the routine to get it—even if the routine is something we'd rather change, like biting nails, smoking, or overeating.

Sometimes, changing a habit is as simple as avoiding the trigger. I remember a season when I stopped at practically any Starbucks coffee shop every morning on my way to work—even though I wasn't in need of a coffee. When the credit card bills showed my spending, I realized I needed to change something. So I took a different route. No trigger, no craving.

But often, that's not enough. We may need to change the action itself. At one point, I was drinking pop or sodas every day. I know—yikes. I analyzed my behaviour and realized the cue was thirst, the action was drinking pop or soda full of sugar and caffeine, and the reward was quenching thirst with a sugar boost. So I stopped buying them and made sure I always had water available. Now I drink water all day. The habit is still there—I just replaced the unhealthy action with a better one. The real reward wasn't sugar; it was hydration.

Another example: if you take a 10 a.m. break with colleagues and drink coffee, but want to cut down on caffeine, you need to identify your rewards. The break is the cue. The actions are socializing and drinking coffee. The rewards are caffeine and oxytocin—the bonding hormone. So what are you really after? If it's socializing, cutting coffee is easy—

just replace it with tea or water. If it's caffeine, find a healthier alternative. If it's about waking up, try going outside for a walk during your break. Start associating your 10 a.m. break with fresh air and movement.

Habits can also be helpful. We can "piggyback" on existing habits—using the action of one habit as a trigger for another. For example, if you don't want to forget something and know you'll be leaving the house later, place a reminder next to your car keys. Picking up your keys becomes the cue, and you'll remember what you need to do.

If you want to create a new habit or change an existing one, start thinking in terms of cue, action, and reward. As you repeat the action following the trigger and receive the reward, your brain begins to rewire itself. Galatians 6:9 encourages us, *"Let us not become weary in doing good, for at the proper time we will reap a harvest if we do not give up."* Persistence matters.

Make things convenient and easy. Your cue should be clearly associated with your action. If you want to run every Saturday morning, keep your running shoes in plain sight. Don't hide them in the closet. If you want to practice yoga, keep your mat nearby and hang a poster of someone doing yoga where you'll see it. Visual cues are powerful reminders.

You can also set alarms on your phone to remind you of the action. The alarm becomes the trigger. Without a clear trigger, there's no action—and no reward.

The key to a successful habit starts with a clear cue. From there, it's about consistency, grace, and understanding how your brain works. And remember: you're not doing this alone. Philippians 4:13 says, *"I can do all things through Christ who strengthens me."* With God's help, even the hardest habits can be transformed.

So take heart. Your habits don't define you. They can be reshaped, renewed, and redeemed—one cue, one action, one reward at a time.

SELF-CONTROL

I know it all sounds great in theory—just say no to temptation, exercise willpower, and live victoriously. But in real life, it doesn't always work that way. Well… actually, sometimes it does. But often, it doesn't. The flesh is weak, and temptation is everywhere. We crave that dopamine hit we know we'll get once we indulge ourselves. In fact, dopamine is already responsible for that craving—that intense feeling of anticipation before we even act.

Sometimes, the only thing standing between our good intentions and instant gratification is willpower. But there's a lot of confusion about what willpower really is. Some people think it means making a big enough effort to summon strength from somewhere deep inside and overcome temptation. But it's not that simple.

There's a balance between the level of external temptation and our ability to delay or avoid indulging in that desire. Sometimes, the temptation in our environment is mild, and we can exercise control.

Other times, it's overwhelming—and we cave. But here's the good news: self-control can be developed. And I want to share how.

Let's say you want to cut down on ice cream. But every time the opportunity presents itself, you give in. In the last chapter, we talked about how habits start with a cue or trigger. In this example, the cue might be walking past your favourite ice cream shop or seeing your favourite flavour in the freezer. That cue leads to the behaviour—buying and eating the ice cream. Often, this behaviour is mindless and beyond conscious control. It's automatic. And the immediate consequence? You feel good. The ice cream tastes amazing. You get your dopamine hit.

One way to deal with this is to avoid acute temptation altogether. But since that's not always possible, how do we develop self-control?

I've learned if you can begin to respond to the cue with a different behaviour—like walking past the shop without buying anything—your brain can learn this new response. The key is: can you exercise that restraint consistently enough to change your brain?

The answer doesn't come just from neuroscience, but also from behavioural therapy—specifically the kind used to help stroke victims regain lost functionality. Call it applied neuroplasticity.

Let's say someone has lost the use of their right hand after a stroke. The way to recovery isn't by trying to move the whole hand at once. That would fail and discourage the patient. Instead, therapists break the movement down into baby steps. First, they try to move the tip of one finger. Then another. Slowly, control is regained.

The same is true with willpower. If you try to resist temptation head-on, you'll likely fail and feel discouraged. So, like a rehabilitation program, we need to break things down into manageable steps.

Step one is to visualize yourself in a tempting situation and successfully gaining the upper hand. Whatever it is you want to change, imagine yourself being victorious. Make it vivid. Picture the details. Feel the emotions. Make it real.

I remember trying to cut back on sugar. My weakness? Ice-cream. I started by imagining myself walking past Dairy Queen without buying any. I pictured the smell, the display, the craving—and then me walking away with peace in my heart. That mental rehearsal helped more than I expected.

Step two might be to look in the ice cream shop window for a few seconds and then walk away. Step three could be going into the shop with friends, agreeing ahead of time that you won't buy anything, and leaving quickly. Step four might be sitting with friends while they eat ice cream and choosing a healthier alternative for yourself.

Each step builds strength. Each victory rewires your brain.

Galatians 5:22–23 reminds us that *"the fruit of the Spirit is love, joy, peace, patience, kindness, goodness, faithfulness, gentleness, and self-control."*

Self-control isn't just a personal achievement—it's a spiritual fruit. It grows in us as we walk with God.

And 1 Corinthians 10:13 offers this promise: *"No temptation has overtaken you except what is common to mankind. And God is faithful; He will not let you be tempted beyond what you can bear. But when you are tempted, He will also provide a way out so that you can endure it."*

That way out might be a baby step. A visualization. A walk past the shop. A prayer whispered in the moment of craving.

So take heart. You're not weak—you're human. And with God's help, you can grow stronger. Self-control isn't about perfection. It's about progress. One cue, one choice, one victory at a time.

THOUGHT *developmental* PRACTICE **(TDP)**

We have tens of thousands of thoughts every day. Some are short-lived, some happen over and over, and some change the way we see ourselves and the world. If you have an addiction, anxiety, or depression, many of these thoughts are not only unhelpful but can also be harmful. They can make you hurt yourself, make bad choices, and use coping methods that only make things worse.

But the truth is that your thoughts aren't set in stone. They can grow, change, and become something else. This process, which we call thought developmental practice, is about learning how to spot negative thought patterns, question them, and replace them with ones that are positive, hopeful, and healing.

Ideas are strong. They affect how we feel, how we act, and what we decide to do. People who use cannabis or other drugs often think, "I can't handle this stress," which leads them to use drugs to deal with it. When someone with depression thinks, "I'm worthless," that thought can lead to being alone or hurting themselves.

These aren't just feelings; they're patterns in the brain. The brain builds pathways based on things we think and do over and over. The more we think about something, the easier it is to do. This is why it's so easy to think negatively: it's been reinforced over time. But these pathways can be changed, just like they were made. We can change the way we think by practicing on purpose. This will help us make better choices, have fewer regrets, and cope with stress in healthier ways.

Awareness is the first step in thought developmental practice. We need to learn how to spot the thoughts that hurt us. These often include thinking that everything is bad, making things personal, thinking that things are either good or bad, feeling hopeless, and making excuses. These thoughts often come to mind when you're feeling weak, like after a mistake, during a fight, or when you're under a lot of stress. They seem real, but they're not. They are wrong, and you can fight them.

After we notice a bad thought, the next thing to do is change how we think about it. This doesn't mean pretending everything is fine; it means finding a more honest and fair way to look at things. Instead of saying, *"I can't handle this,"* say, *"This is hard, but I've been through hard things before."* Say, *"I made a mistake, but I'm learning and growing"* instead of *"I'm a failure."* Say, *"I'm learning to use healthier ways to cope,"* instead of *"I need to use to feel better."*

Cognitive restructuring is the name of this process, and it's a big part of therapy that helps people get better. It helps people replace negative thoughts with positive ones, which lowers the chance of relapse and makes it easier to control their emotions.

Optimism isn't just something you are; it's something you can learn. And just like any other skill, it can be learned. Practices like gratitude journaling, positive affirmations, visualization, and mindfulness can help your brain learn to expect good things, see possibilities, and respond with hope. These things help you change your focus from not having enough to having plenty, from being afraid to being faithful, and from being hopeless to being strong.

Regret is a strong feeling. It often happens after making rash choices, especially when drugs or strong feelings are involved. When you feel bad about yourself, it can make you do things that hurt yourself even more.

We need to learn to stop in order to break this cycle. If you think something like "*I need to get away*" or "*I can't take this*," stop. Take a breath. Think about how you feel. What do I need? How can I respond in a healthier way? "This pause gives you room to make a choice." It is where change starts.

This break is very important for people who are having trouble with cannabis or other drugs. People often turn to drugs or alcohol when they're uncomfortable. But feeling bad isn't a sign of death; it's a signal. It means "*I need care*" from the body. Thought developmental practice teaches us to respond with kindness instead of avoiding it.

Anxiety and depression change the way we think. They make the future seem scary and the present seem empty. But even in these situations, it's still possible to develop your thoughts. If you're feeling anxious, focus on what you can control, question catastrophic thoughts, and use grounding techniques to stay in the moment. Set small, doable goals, celebrate your progress, and reach out to others, even when it's hard, if you're depressed.

It's not about being perfect; it's about sticking with it. You make a new path stronger every time you choose a healthier thought. You get your mind back every time you stop yourself from sabotaging yourself.

You don't have to do this by yourself. It's hard work to develop your thoughts, but it's easier with help. Talk about your journey with a therapist, a recovery group, or a friend you trust. When your own thoughts are too heavy, let other people speak the truth into your life. Practices that focus on recovery stress dignity, hope, and giving people power. They remind us that healing is possible and that everyone, no matter what they're going through, deserves love and change.

Your thoughts have a big impact on your life. But your thoughts don't define you. You are the one who thinks. And that means you can change them. Thought developmental practice is about getting that power back. It's about picking hope over despair, truth over lies, and healing over hurting. Your mind can be renewed, even if you have an addiction, anxiety, or depression. Your story can change.

I created the Thought Developmental Practice (TDP) research, which has been shown to change the way people think and recondition their minds. It creates a distraction to help the brain make new neural pathways, like teaching the less dominant hand to write with it. Changing negative thoughts into positive ones and using a few different methods to help people deal with stress.

Thought Developmental Practice (TDP) is a well-known and effective way to treat addiction, anxiety and depression. It is a structured, time-limited, and goal-oriented psychotherapeutic approach that focuses on identifying, understanding, and changing thinking and behaviour patterns.

TDP is based on the idea that thoughts, feelings, and actions are all connected and that changing one can change the others. One of the main ideas of TDP in addiction is to find negative thought patterns. TDP helps people see and question thoughts that are wrong or don't make sense that lead to drug use. It also helps to keep the cravings that come with the thought pattern at bay. Someone might think they need a drug to deal with stress, but TDP can help change those cravings by giving them a lot of different things to do.

TDP helps us make positive changes in our behaviour by giving us different things to do when we want something. This could mean learning new ways to deal with stress, staying away from things that make you want to use drugs, or making healthier choices in your daily life.

TDP teaches people how to deal with cravings and stay sober. This includes ways to handle stress, control your feelings, and get better at talking to people. TDP helps the mind get used to healthy ways of dealing with stress that can become a way of life.

TDP improves people's ability to solve problems, which helps them deal with problems and setbacks in a more positive way and makes it less likely that they will turn to drugs or alcohol to solve them.

There has been a lot of research on TDP, and it has been shown to work for a number of substance use disorders and those struggling with anxiety and depression. The skills learned through TDP stay with the person long after treatment ends, which helps them stay sober for a long time.

TDP for addiction is often most effective when integrated with complementary treatment modalities. This comprehensive approach acknowledges the complex nature of addiction as a disorder affecting individuals on biological, psychological, and social levels.

Combining TDP with medication-assisted treatment (MAT) is a key part of this integration. People who are addicted to drugs like alcohol or opioids that have a strong physical component can use MAT to help them deal with withdrawal symptoms and cravings.

When MAT is used with TDP, the medicine makes the patient or client feel better physically. This helps them do the exercises better to change the way they think and recondition their minds by using distraction techniques. This combination looks at both the biological and psychological reasons why people become addicted and the behaviours and thought patterns that keep them using drugs.

Combining TDP with other treatments can also help people who have more than one mental health problem, like anxiety or depression. People who are addicted to drugs or alcohol often have other mental health problems that may have led to their substance use disorder. Integrating TDP with therapies aimed at these co-occurring disorders can offer a more holistic treatment strategy, encompassing all aspects of the individual's health.

It is a tool that helps people understand their own thoughts and feelings and the relationships they have with other people. The process helps people move on from problems that came up in the past and make new, positive memory cards to replace the old, bad ones.

The goal of TDP is not to get rid of emotions or the way a person thinks, but to give them more ways to deal with problems by giving them useful, positive ideas. It aims to help people use what they already know and do to help themselves and others. The main goal of TDP is to help people find the root causes of their unhappiness by getting rid of bad habits, thoughts, and ideas and replacing them with value-based ideas that make them feel good about themselves.

The process of examining causes, effects, and solutions begins, aiming to pinpoint and surmount the emotional and cognitive barriers hindering advancement. For example, if a patient or client uses drugs or alcohol to deal with stress, TDP can help them learn better ways to deal with stress. For someone whose substance use is related to social anxiety, the therapy can also teach them how to deal with anxiety in social situations.

If you are interested in developing your thoughts, stimulating the brain, and creating healthy mental diversions—especially for those struggling with addictions, anxiety, or depression—there is a structured approach called Thought Development Practice that may be of great benefit. This method is designed to help individuals rewire their thinking patterns, strengthen emotional regulation, and foster resilience through intentional cognitive exercises.

To fully engage with this practice, participants are encouraged to commit to a 12-week course that guides them through the process of rewiring the brain. The course is grounded in the principles of neuroplasticity and psychological healing, offering practical tools to reshape thought patterns and promote mental wellness.

A comprehensive workbook accompanies the course, developed collaboratively by myself and a team of researchers under the supervision of Dr. David Koczerginski, Chief of Psychiatry and Medical Director of Mental Health. This resource includes evidence-based strategies, reflective exercises, and guided practices tailored to support individuals on their journey toward clarity, emotional strength, and recovery.

Whether you're a clinician seeking new tools for your clients or someone navigating personal challenges, Thought Development Practice offers a hopeful and scientifically informed path forward.

NEUROGENISIS

We need to let go of the things that are holding us back in order to be happy. We can do this by creating new neuropathy that can replace our old bad habits, negative thoughts, regrets, and emotional wounds. We are about to learn something new: how amazing our brains are at adapting and changing.

We need to know more about how the brain can change and grow. We need to go on an exciting trip to learn more about our neural pathways and what they can do. It will show how amazing neuroplasticity is—the brain's ability to change shape, make new connections, and have a big impact on our lives.

We need to learn how to use all of our brain's power and how being able to change can help us have better lives, relationships, and futures. As we learn about all the amazing things that neuroplasticity can do, we should be ready for them.

Neurogenesis, or the process of making new brain cells, is very interesting because it shows how well the brain can heal itself. People used to think that an adult's brain didn't change. Our brains are very good at making new neurons all the time. This news gives us hope for a fresh start—a chance for our minds to heal, change, and grow.

Neurogenesis is the study of how neural stem cells develop and change. These cells can turn into different kinds of brain cells, like neurons, which is really cool. These neural stem cells are in some parts of the brain, like the hippocampus, which is very important for learning, memory, and controlling emotions. These stem cells divide, turn into different types of cells, and grow up in a very planned way. They make new neurons that fit right in with the neural circuitry that is already there.

Neurogenesis doesn't only create new cells. These new neurons can change and grow in ways that make them very aware of what's going on around them. They become part of the complicated web of neural connections that helps change and rewire neural circuits. This helps people learn new things and look at things in new ways.

Neurogenesis is very important for our health and happiness. It is important for a lot of mental processes, like learning, remembering things, and seeing patterns. Neurogenesis is also closely linked to mental health and how well you can handle your emotions. It might make people less sad and anxious and make them stronger overall.

It's a good thing that there are some good ways to promote neurogenesis and keep your brain healthy. Exercise, for instance, has been shown to be a strong promoter of neurogenesis. Swimming, jogging, and biking are all examples of aerobic exercises that are good for your heart and lungs. They also help your brain make new neurons in the hippocampus, which is where memories are kept.

Eating a balanced diet that includes all the right nutrients, getting enough sleep, learning how to deal with stress, and keeping your mind busy can all help create an environment that is good for neurogenesis. Eating foods high in omega-3 fatty acids, like fish, and fruits and vegetables, which are high in antioxidants, can help your brain work better and make new brain cells.

Your brain works harder when you learn a new language, play an instrument, or solve puzzles. This is good for neurogenesis because it helps your brain learn new things and connect with other things. We can start to grow and change as people by using these methods and encouraging the growth of new neurons. Making the world around us better can help our brains heal. This will help us stop doing things the way we've always done them and be open to all the ways we can change.

Over time, our brains have built complicated networks of neurons that connect our thoughts, habits, and responses. These neural networks are the pathways that information travels, altering our perceptions and behaviours. But not all of these patterns are good for us. Some of them come from things that happened in the past, and they are very strong.

They often keep us from growing and being happy. It's very important to know how much these neural networks that are already in place affect our lives. They tell us what to do and what to think without us even thinking about it. They even change the beliefs that are most important to us. These habits and beliefs that tell us we don't deserve love or that keep us from moving forward can be hard to break.

But there is hope for change deep down in our brains. Neuroplasticity is the brain's amazing ability to change and move things around. This lets us change these neural networks and get rid of habits that aren't good for us anymore.

By paying attention to them, we can find the neural networks that make up our thoughts, habits, and reactions. By recognizing things, we can figure out where our patterns came from and how they have changed our lives. Because we know this, we can now start to change how our brains work.

You need to actively question whether negative patterns are true and replace them with new beliefs and actions that give you strength. We need to deal with the voice in our heads that tells us we're not good enough and replace it with a voice that is nice and helpful.

Cognitive restructuring makes it very easy to change how neural networks work. We can change the way we think by carefully examining our thoughts and making sure they are true. This process involves identifying cognitive distortions, such as dichotomous thinking or catastrophizing, and replacing them with more balanced and practical thoughts.

We should use the power of pictures and good thoughts that we have. By saying nice things about ourselves over and over and picturing the results we want, we can create new neural pathways that help us think and act in ways that give us power. Through repetition and consistency, these new patterns get stronger and slowly take the place of the old, limiting ones.

To change how our brains work, we need to be willing to try new things and step outside of our comfort zones. When we try new things, learn new skills, or look at things from a different angle, our brains change and adapt to the new information. This process of synaptic pruning and strengthening of relevant connections enables us to think, act, and perceive in novel ways.

Changing how neural networks work takes time. You need to be patient, keep going, and be nice to yourself. When we try to change our habits, things don't always go as planned, and we may have to start over. But if we stay focused on our growth and use neuroplasticity, we can slowly break free from the limits of the past and make new neural networks that will help us reach our goal of a happy and fulfilling future.

We need to take an exciting trip into the world of neuroscience to learn about the interesting processes of neurogenesis and neural adaptation. We'll learn how to be more open-minded and stop doing things the same way. This will give us the strength and grace to handle the changes that life throws at us.

We should also look into how neuroplasticity is linked to mental health. This could help us figure out how to use our minds to heal old wounds and turn bad things into good things. We should learn more about how mindfulness, cognitive enhancers, and the social environment can help us with the rewiring process by giving us useful tools and information along the way.

Keep in mind that neuroplasticity can help you change your neuropathy. Don't worry; open your heart and mind to all the good things that could happen. Say no to the past and use the power of your brain to change as we begin this amazing journey together.

The brain is a great example of how things can grow and change. It has billions of neurons, and they are all connected in a very complicated way. Neuroplasticity is the phenomenon that has changed the way we think about how the brain works. This amazing ability is based on it. Neuroplasticity is the brain's incredible ability to change itself by forming new neural connections and pathways in response to your actions, thoughts, and emotions.

For instance, think of someone who is learning how to play an instrument. The task might seem too hard at first, the notes might sound strange, and the way you move your fingers might not feel right. But when you do something over and over, your brain does something amazing. The neurons that process the music start to connect with each other in new ways, which makes it easier for them to work together to move the instrument. Over time, the brain changes so that this new skill becomes second nature. This shows that the brain can change.

The concept of brain plasticity is crucial for emotional resilience. It's amazing how our brains can change, rewire, and make new connections between neurons at any point in our lives. We can change our thoughts, feelings, and actions in ways that used to seem like they would last forever. This helps us learn new ways to handle things that help us grow.

Learning how to control your feelings is one of the best ways to use brain plasticity to make yourself stronger emotionally. We can change how strong and long our feelings are by learning about them and controlling them. This helps us feel better and more balanced. Meditation, deep breathing, and writing in a journal are all great ways to learn how to control your feelings. These things help us understand and accept how we feel without judging them. This helps us get through tough times in a calmer and more helpful way.

We need to be nice, understanding, forgiving, and caring to ourselves. It's fine to mess up and realize that we aren't perfect. When we treat ourselves the same way we would treat someone we care about, we get better at handling stress and our emotional health.

To become emotionally stronger, you need to use your brain's ability to change. This type of psychology is all about finding and building on strengths, good feelings, and a sense of purpose and meaning in life. By actively cultivating feelings like gratitude, joy, and hope, we can change how our brains work to look for and make good experiences stronger, even when things are hard.

Being grateful, doing things that make us happy, and spending time with people we care about are all great ways to boost our mood and make us stronger emotionally. Remember that brain plasticity is an ongoing process that helps you become more emotionally strong. You have to be patient, practice, and be determined to learn a skill. Every day, we change how our brains work by using positive psychology, being kind to ourselves, and using emotional regulation techniques. This makes us stronger emotionally and becomes a part of who we are.

As we go through this life-changing journey, let's be grateful for how well our brains can change and adapt. We can use the brain's ability to change to make ourselves stronger emotionally. This will help us deal with the problems in life with grace, strength, and a strong sense of well-being. Let's go on this journey of empowerment together, changing the way we think and making room for a future full of happiness and emotional strength.

When something bad happens to us, our brains do things right away to keep us safe. But these changes can last long after the threat has passed, and they can make it hard to think, feel, and stay healthy.

Learning how trauma affects the brain is a big part of getting better. When we're really stressed, the amygdala, which is the part of the brain that sounds the alarm, works too hard. This starts a chain of events that gets us ready to fight, run away, or stay where we are. This higher level of reactivity can lead to many issues, including anxiety, hypervigilance, and emotional numbness.

As we work to change how our brains work, we will always see improvements in neuroplasticity. One of the best ways to keep positive change going is to make new habits, behaviours, and ways of thinking a part of our daily lives. Change can be exciting at first, but what really makes the rewiring process work is sticking with these new ways of being. We need to make a detailed plan for how to fit these changes into our lives every day.

COGNITIVE
FLEXIBILITY

Cognitive flexibility means that your mind can switch between thinking about different things, accepting new information, and changing your plans or beliefs when circumstances change. It's not just a skill—it's a way of looking at things. It helps people deal with confusion, doubt, and contradictions without becoming overly stressed or stuck. Cognitive flexibility is the ability to stay focused and coherent while still being able to change your mind.

This quality is essential for solving problems, being creative, managing emotions, and getting along with others. A flexible thinker can view situations from different perspectives, tolerate uncertainty, and revise their thinking when needed. They are not trapped in rigid patterns or outdated habits. Instead, they respond to situations as they arise, adjusting their approach without losing their sense of identity.

Cognitive flexibility is closely related to executive functioning, especially in the prefrontal cortex. It involves working memory, impulse control, and the ability to shift mental sets. These processes help a person retain multiple pieces of information, inhibit automatic responses, and switch between tasks or viewpoints. This might mean changing your opinion after hearing new evidence, adjusting how you communicate with different people, or finding alternative solutions when a plan fails.

Being able to change your mind also supports emotional resilience. A mind that is open to new ideas can reframe failure or loss, find meaning in it, and move forward. It doesn't ignore pain—it integrates it. This integration allows for growth. People with high cognitive flexibility tend to recover from setbacks more quickly because they can shift from blame to learning and from dwelling on the past to planning for the future.

Cognitive flexibility enhances understanding and cooperation in relationships. It helps you empathize with others, adjust expectations, and respond thoughtfully instead of reacting impulsively. It's the difference between wanting to be right and being willing to learn. Open-minded individuals are better collaborators because they can negotiate, compromise, and generate new ideas together.

Cognitive rigidity, on the other hand, is characterized by black-and-white thinking, resistance to change, and difficulty adapting. It often stems from fear—fear of the unknown, fear of being wrong, or fear of losing control. While rigidity may feel safe, it hinders growth. It prevents people from exploring new ideas and makes it harder to cope with challenges.

There are several ways to strengthen cognitive flexibility. First, cultivate curiosity—ask questions, try new things, and challenge your assumptions. Second, practice mindfulness—become aware of your thoughts and feelings without judgment. This creates space for intentional choices. Third, view failure as feedback rather than a verdict. Every mistake becomes an opportunity to learn and adjust.

Seeing things from different angles also promotes open-mindedness. You can expand your thinking by reading widely, engaging in conversations, and exploring new environments. The more diverse the input, the more nuanced the output. This doesn't mean abandoning your beliefs—it means refining them. An open mind is not empty; it is receptive.

Cognitive flexibility is a skill that helps you survive when things are changing quickly—whether in your own life, in society, or in technology. It allows you to adapt without falling apart. It helps people stay grounded even as circumstances shift. It's the difference between bending and breaking.

A great example of this is the story of Paul in Acts 16. Paul and his companions are doing ministry work, but the Holy Spirit stops them from going to Bithynia and Asia. Twice, their plans are blocked. They don't resist or push their own agenda; they remain open. That night, Paul has a vision of a man from Macedonia asking for help. They change direction immediately. This is cognitive flexibility in action: the ability to shift based on what the Spirit reveals—not out of uncertainty, but out of faith.

Paul's willingness to change his plans shows his openness to divine intervention. Because of this flexibility, churches grow in Berea, Thessalonica, and Philippi. The gospel spreads because Paul is willing to change.

Isaiah 55 says, "*My thoughts are not your thoughts, and your ways are not my ways.*" This verse calls us to humility and openness to changing our minds. It reminds us that God's logic isn't always what we expect.

To walk with God means being open to change, letting go of control, and embracing the unknown. In this way, cognitive flexibility isn't just quick thinking—it's surrendering the freedom of our minds. It's the willingness to be amazed by grace, led by truth, and transformed by love. God's word, like rain and snow falling to the ground, never returns empty. It accomplishes His purpose, though not always in the way we imagine.

Numbers 27 shows how the daughters of Zelophehad change the course of history by asking for something bold. Their father dies without sons, so they ask Moses for his inheritance. This request is unprecedented. Moses brings their case to God, and God agrees: "*What Zelophehad's daughters are saying is right.*" This marks a turning point in inheritance law, driven by courageous advocacy and

God's swift response. The daughters' willingness to challenge tradition and Moses' openness to new ideas demonstrate strong faith. Here, cognitive flexibility leads to justice and inclusion. It shows that God's law can evolve in response to the needs of His people.

When Jesus speaks with the Syrophoenician woman in Mark 7, He shows remarkable openness. He begins with a metaphor about children and dogs, implying His mission is first to Israel. But the woman replies, "*Even the dogs under the table eat the children's crumbs.*" Jesus heals her daughter because of her wit and persistence.

This exchange reveals a moment when Jesus' ministry expands because He is willing to extend more grace. The woman's faith prompts Jesus to shift the conversation. This story illustrates how open-minded dialogue can lead to breakthroughs, and how humility can bring healing.

Joseph's life also exemplifies cognitive flexibility. He doesn't become bitter or hardened after his brothers betray him, sell him into slavery, and he's imprisoned unjustly. Instead, he adapts. He interprets dreams, manages resources, and eventually becomes ruler of Egypt.

When his brothers come seeking food, he tests them, forgives them, and rewrites the story: "*You meant to harm me, but God meant it for good.*" Joseph's ability to view his suffering through the lens of God's plan reflects profound flexibility. He doesn't deny the pain, but he refuses to be defined by it. He sees the good that can emerge from hardship.

Proverbs 18:13 says, "*To answer before listening—that is folly and shame.*" This verse highlights the importance of open-mindedness in conversation. Listening requires putting aside our own assumptions and being receptive to new perspectives.

A rigid mind reacts impulsively, while a flexible mind listens carefully. This principle applies to our interactions with others and with God. Prayer isn't just speaking—it's listening. Discernment isn't just knowledge—it's patience. Cognitive flexibility allows us to pause, reflect, and respond wisely rather than react hastily.

The book of Ecclesiastes celebrates mental openness. "*There is a time for everything,*" it says. A time to plant and a time to uproot, a time to weep and a time to laugh. This rhythmic wisdom urges us to release the illusion of permanence, embrace change, and move with the seasons.

The author doesn't offer formulas—he offers tensions. He understands that life is full of surprises, and that adaptability is a mark of wisdom. Here, cognitive flexibility means staying true to yourself while navigating change, and accepting both joy and sorrow, gain and loss.

"*Think about what I'm saying,*" Paul writes in 2 Timothy 2:7. "*The Lord will help you understand all this.*" To reflect is to think in a way that welcomes change. It means revisiting ideas, reconsidering them, and seeing them in a new light.

Understanding doesn't always come instantly; sometimes it takes time. An open mind doesn't leap to conclusions—it makes room for revelation. Paul's invitation to reflect is an invitation to grow—to let the Spirit reveal truth gradually. Spiritual growth requires this kind of thinking. It resists dogma and embraces discovery.

Cognitive flexibility doesn't mean abandoning conviction—it means deepening understanding. It's the ability to hold both truth and mystery, staying anchored while remaining open to transformation.

You see this balance in Jesus' life. He honours the law but reinterprets it. He respects tradition but questions it. He speaks with authority but listens with compassion. His mind isn't rigid—it's radiant and attuned to the Father's voice. He understands people's needs and is willing to change for love.

Life is always changing, so our happiness and growth depend on our ability to adapt. Cognitive flexibility is a vital skill that helps us navigate life's ups and downs. It means adjusting how we think, perceive, and act when we encounter new information or changing circumstances. It helps us break free from rigid patterns and embrace new ideas, perspectives, and solutions.

Cognitive flexibility isn't just a thought—it shapes how we feel and act every day. When we think creatively, we become more resilient and better equipped to handle change. It helps us face surprises and see change as an opportunity for growth rather than a threat.

We can respond to life's challenges more effectively by shifting our mindset and behavior when things don't go as planned. We experience greater freedom and possibility when we change how we think. This opens new paths and helps us exceed our own expectations.

One way to cultivate open-mindedness is to reframe situations. Reframing means consciously choosing to see things differently. We can view problems as opportunities for learning and growth rather than as obstacles. We can reinterpret hardships as lessons or blessings in disguise. This shift expands our options.

Trying new things and stepping outside our comfort zones also strengthens cognitive flexibility. Visiting unfamiliar places, experimenting with new activities, or engaging in creative pursuits stimulates our brains and encourages fresh thinking. Openness to novelty and uncertainty fosters learning and innovation.

It's important to remember that developing cognitive flexibility takes time and practice. Be gentle and patient with yourself along the way. Celebrate each small step forward. As we become more adaptable, we gain more choices, more power, and more joy. Let go of stubbornness and watch your life transform.

Emotional resilience also depends on the ability to adapt and persevere. It's a crucial trait that helps us face life's challenges with strength and courage. The intensity of our emotions is closely tied to the brain's capacity for change.

Learning to regulate our feelings helps us understand how neuroplasticity supports emotional well-being. Embracing cognitive flexibility not only improves our ability to handle change—it also strengthens us emotionally. We've learned to harness brain plasticity to enhance mental health. This has helped us recover from adversity and remain hopeful. Our brains are now more adaptable, helping us stay positive even in difficult times.

When someone gives their mind to God, it becomes a place where they can be renewed, learn, and creatively obey. It shows how God wants His people to be open to new ideas, respond wisely, and remain receptive to His evolving plans.

In 1 Samuel 25, Abigail shows she can think on her feet when things get tough. Her husband, Nabal, has insulted David, and now David is coming to retaliate. Abigail doesn't deny the situation or panic. Instead, she quickly recognizes the danger, gathers supplies, and intercepts David with a plea for peace.

She is wise and humble, shifting from household chores to diplomatic intervention. She reframes the situation—not by denying reality, but by offering David a new perspective that honours his calling and prevents violence. *"Let the blame be on me alone,"* she says, showing her willingness to bear stress in pursuit of resolution. Abigail's story demonstrates that changing your mind is not impulsiveness—it is Spirit-led discernment.

God gives an unnamed prophet a man of God from Judah in 1 Kings 13 specific instructions: deliver a message and return immediately. But when an older prophet lies and claims divine authority, the younger prophet changes his mind and eats with him. The result is tragic—a lion kills him on the road. This story teaches that flexibility isn't always wise. The prophet's change was based on persuasion, not discernment.

True cognitive flexibility can distinguish between divine guidance and human manipulation. A mind attuned to God's voice stays open to new ideas while holding fast to truth. This story reminds us how easily relationships or misplaced trust can cloud spiritual clarity.

In 2 Chronicles 20, Jehoshaphat faces a coalition of enemies. He doesn't rely solely on military strategy; he calls the people to pray and listens to prophetic counsel. The Spirit speaks through Jahaziel, declaring that the Lord will fight the battle. Jehoshaphat doesn't arm his soldiers—instead, he appoints singers to lead the army in worship.

This dramatic shift—from fear to praise, from swords to songs—reveals faith-based cognitive flexibility. The king's decision to abandon conventional wisdom and follow God's plan secures victory. The enemies turn on each other, and Judah is spared. This story shows that faith opens the door to miracles.

In Acts 16, the Holy Spirit prevents Paul and his companions from preaching in Asia. They try again to enter Bithynia, but the Spirit stops them. That night, Paul has a vision of a man from Macedonia asking for help. They immediately change course.

Paul is receptive to God's guidance because he's willing to revise his plans. His cognitive flexibility leads to the founding of churches in Philippi, Thessalonica, and Berea. The lesson is that a mind open to new direction is a mind that hears. Plans are good, but obedience is better. When the Spirit intervenes, wise people don't resist—they prepare.

Job's friends speak at length, clinging to a rigid belief that suffering is punishment for sin. Elihu, the youngest among them, disagrees. In Job 32, he offers a more nuanced view of divine justice, marked by humility and insight. He says, *"It is not only the old who are wise, not only the aged who understand what is right."*

Elihu's openness allows him to speak truth and challenge expectations. His perspective creates space for deeper reflection and prepares the way for God's voice. In this case, wisdom is not about age—it's about openness. Elihu's fresh insight breaks the cycle of blame and opens the door to healing.

In Luke 13, Jesus heals a woman who had been paralyzed for eighteen years. He does this on the Sabbath, which angers the religious leaders. They cling to tradition, but Jesus redefines the Sabbath—not just as a day of rest, but as a day of healing. He asks, *"Shouldn't this woman, a daughter of Abraham, whom Satan has kept bound for eighteen long years, be set free on the Sabbath day?"* His question invites flexible thinking, shifting from rigidity to compassion.

The leaders miss the miracle because they refuse to change. Jesus teaches that true understanding of Scripture requires a theology rooted in love and open to transformation. When the Sabbath is rightly understood, it becomes a day of restoration.

To walk with God is to embrace the unknown, relinquish control, and remain ready to change. In this way, cognitive flexibility is not just mental agility—it is spiritual surrender. It is the willingness to be amazed by grace, led by truth, and transformed by love.

RECONDITION *The* MIND

The mind is a strong place where people can heal, grow, and change. People who have been through trauma, abuse, addiction, or mental health problems can also have pain in their minds. After pain, racing thoughts, negative self-talk, and unwanted intrusive thoughts often begin to occur. It seems like this cycle will never end. Reconditioning the mind does not mean forgetting the past or pretending that pain doesn't exist; instead, it means changing the way we think in a gentle and planned way to help us heal.

The brain changes to help people who have been hurt or abused survive. It becomes hypervigilant and looks for danger even when there isn't any. Thoughts race because the nervous system is on high alert. When people are told, directly or indirectly, that they are not worthy, safe, or powerful, they start to believe bad things about themselves. These ways of thinking aren't bad things about you; they're ways to stay alive. But once the threat is gone, these patterns can make it hard to relax.

A lot of the time, people use drugs or alcohol to help them deal with these strong thoughts and feelings. Cannabis, alcohol, and opioids are drugs that can help with pain and calm the mind for a short time. But over time, they make the patterns they were supposed to calm even stronger. Instead of looking for ways to solve problems, the mind learns to look for ways to get away. Reconditioning the mind means teaching it to react differently, not by avoiding things, but by being aware, caring, and making choices.

Romans 12:2 became my anchor: *"Do not conform to the pattern of this world, but be transformed by the renewing of your mind."* That verse isn't just poetic—it's practical. It told me that transformation starts in the mind. I began to notice how often my thoughts defaulted to scarcity, fear, and self-doubt.

So I started speaking truth over myself. I didn't feel strong, but I said, *"I can do all things through Christ who strengthens me"* (Philippians 4:13). I didn't feel secure, but I said, *"God has not given me a spirit of fear, but of power, love, and a sound mind"* (2 Timothy 1:7). These weren't just affirmations—they were spiritual recalibrations.

David did this constantly. In Psalm 42, he says, *"Why, my soul, are you downcast? Why so disturbed within me? Put your hope in God..."* He talks to himself. He redirects his mind. That's reconditioning.

I've done the same—especially when grief or exhaustion tries to take over. I've learned to pause and ask, *"Is this thought true? Is it noble? Is it lovely?"* (Philippians 4:8). That verse became my filter. And the more I used it, the more my mind began to shift.

Jesus reconditioned minds too. When He healed the paralytic in Matthew 9, He didn't start with the body—He started with the heart: *"Take heart, son; your sins are forgiven."* He knew that healing begins in the mind. I've seen this in mentoring others.

When someone believes they're broken beyond repair, no advice will help until that belief is challenged. But when they begin to see themselves as beloved, capable, and called, everything changes. Their posture shifts. Their choices shift. Their relationships heal.

Paul's letters are full of this kind of mental renewal. In Colossians 3:2, he says, *"Set your minds on things above, not on earthly things."* That's a daily discipline. I've had to do it in the middle of chaos—when bills pile up, when deadlines loom, when emotions run high.

I've had to lift my thoughts above the noise and anchor them in truth. And when I do, I become more peaceful, more present, more patient. That's the impact on others. My renewed mind creates a safe space for theirs.

Reconditioning the mind is not just personal—it's relational. When I think differently, I speak differently. I listen more deeply. I respond more gently. I lead more wisely. My children feel it. My wife Kathleen feel it. My readers feel it. The renewal in me becomes a refuge for them.

So I keep renewing. I keep surrendering old patterns. I keep choosing truth. Because every time I do, I become more of who God made me to be—and that version of me can love more deeply, serve more freely, and lead more faithfully.

The first thing to do is to notice. If your mind is racing, you're feeling bad, or you're having intrusive thoughts or memories, the first thing to do is to stop and look. "I'm having a lot of thoughts right now." "This feels like too much." "I'm remembering something that hurt." Putting a name to the experience makes a space between the thought and the self.

It reminds us that our thoughts don't define us; we are the ones who see them.

From this place of awareness, we can begin to question and change the way we think. This doesn't mean forcing people to be happy or ignoring the truth. It means asking questions. "Is this thought right?" "Does it help?" "Where did it come from?" "What would I say to someone I love who was thinking this?" These questions make you think about other things. They are open to new ideas.

Reconditioning the mind also means working on the body for people who have been through trauma. Not only does trauma stay in memory, but it also stays in muscles, breathing, and posture. The body and brain are very connected. Some things that can help the nervous system work better are deep breathing, grounding exercises, and gentle movement. These things make it easier to stay calm and think clearly. When the body feels safe, the mind starts to follow.

Being kind to yourself is important. Many people who have racing or bad thoughts also feel bad about themselves. They think they aren't good enough, broken, or weak. But being nice is the first step to getting better. When you talk to yourself, be nice to yourself. These words might seem strange at first, but they will start to make sense over time: "It's okay to feel this way," "I'm doing the best I can," and "I deserve peace." The brain learns how to relax.

Reconditioning also means making new mental habits. You can teach your mind to expect peace, just like you can teach it to expect chaos or pain. Every day, writing in a journal, meditating, praying, or saying nice things can help your brain make new connections. These routines don't have to be perfect or long; they just have to happen every day. Over time, they become anchors that keep the mind safe.

Keep in mind that this process isn't going to be easy. There will be issues. Some days, your mind will be louder than ever. But that doesn't mean you didn't do well. It means that the brain is still getting better. Every time you choose to be aware instead of reacting, to be kind instead of critical, and to be present instead of panicking, you are changing how you think. You are changing.

Reconditioning your mind means taking back control of your thoughts and feelings. It's about letting your brain know that you can be safe and that you deserve peace. It's about getting rid of the old scripts that make you feel ashamed and afraid and replacing them with new ones that make you feel hopeful and respected. Your mind can change, whether you're dealing with trauma, addiction, anxiety, or depression. Your story can change.

Start by taking a breath. One thought. A single act of kindness. And keep going. The mind can get better. And you are too.

Having a positive attitude can be very helpful in this fast-paced and often hard world. It makes us healthier as a group and also gives us the strength to handle life's ups and downs with grace and strength. "Rewiring your brain" works a lot better when you train your mind to stay positive and hopeful.

Having a positive attitude is very strong. It changes how we think, how we feel, and what we do. We can do anything we want when we choose to be positive. Problems turn into chances, and failures turn into steps toward growth and success. But it takes work and a promise to get better to keep this kind of mindset.

We need to learn more about the science behind how to train our minds to be more positive and how to change our thoughts and beliefs so that we see life in a more positive light. We need to find helpful ways and strategies to help us deal with and change negative thoughts, make gratitude a part of our daily lives, and accept failure as a necessary step toward success.

We should also think about how important it is to talk to ourselves in a positive way and how that can change our lives. Talking to ourselves in a positive and supportive way can help us feel better, give us more confidence, and strengthen our sense of self-belief.

We should learn how to be happy. We often worry about what might go wrong in the future or remember what went wrong in the past. This makes us miss the chances and beauty that are right in front of us. Mindfulness and accepting the present can help us enjoy the small things in life more.

We also need to think about how important it is to do things that really make us happy and fulfilled. Taking care of ourselves and doing things we love not only makes us feel better, but it also makes us healthier overall. Also, the power of forgiveness and letting go, and how letting go of old grudges can help us feel better.

Being positive can help us in many ways, such as with our relationships and our overall happiness. We can fill our lives with hope, strength, and a deep love for the journey if we change how we think and focus on the possibilities and potential in every situation.

You have to work on being positive all the time to stay that way. We need helpful tips and tricks that we can use every day to help us make being positive a habit instead of just a mood that comes and goes. Taking care of our minds and learning to stay positive can lead to a lifetime of happiness and fulfillment.

A key part of training your mind to be more positive is learning to see failure as a step toward success. We often think of failure as a flaw in ourselves or a permanent setback, which can make it harder for us to grow and get back on track. But if we see failure as a chance to learn and a normal part of the path to success, we can stop being afraid and start being more positive. People who see failure as a temporary setback and stay positive are more likely to keep going and reach their goals.

It's very important to talk to yourself in a positive way to retrain your mind to be positive. The way we talk to ourselves can change how we feel, what we believe, and how we act. We can feel better about ourselves and gain confidence by consciously replacing negative self-talk and self-criticism with language that is supportive, kind, and empowering. Self-affirmation research shows that saying nice things to yourself can help you relax, get more done, and do better in many areas of life.

A positive attitude can have a huge impact on our lives and the way we see the world. It shapes our thoughts, feelings, and actions, as well as how we see things and how healthy we are overall. We need to look at how a positive attitude affects many parts of our lives to understand how strong it is. It will give us hope and strength to face problems and challenges. We won't let problems get us down; instead, we'll see them as chances to learn and get better. The best way for us to get through problems and reach our goals is to be able to find solutions and keep going.

Psychology, neuroscience, and cognitive behavioural therapy are the scientific fields that explain how to change the way your mind works to be more positive. These areas teach us a lot about how our thoughts, feelings, and actions are all linked. They also teach us how to understand and use the power of a positive attitude.

Also, having a good attitude is good for our mental health. We tend to be happier, more grateful, and more content when we have a positive attitude. These good feelings spread to other people and change our mood, making us feel better mentally and emotionally. We can feel better and get rid of bad feelings by thinking about the good things in our lives.

A good attitude makes our relationships and interactions with other people better. When we are kind and warm to others, we make a good space that helps us get to know them better. People are drawn to us because we have a positive attitude, which makes our relationships stronger. By staying positive, we can make and keep connections that make our lives better.

To get your mind ready for good thoughts, it's important to challenge and change bad ones. We often think about or expect bad things to happen, which can make us feel sad. But we can use cognitive restructuring and other methods to question the truth and accuracy of negative thoughts and replace them with more realistic and positive ones. This process involves closely examining the evidence that supports and goes against negative beliefs, recognizing cognitive distortions, and choosing thoughts that are more positive and empowering on purpose.

Also, doing things that make us happy and fulfilled is very good for our health and well-being. Dopamine and endorphins are chemicals that our brains release when we do things that are fun and important to us. These chemicals are linked to feelings of happiness and pleasure. Doing things like this on a regular basis not only makes us feel better, but it also helps us think positively by reminding us that we deserve happiness and fulfillment.

Our thoughts have a big impact on how we feel, how we act, and how healthy we are in general. Negative thoughts can stop us from reaching our full potential, make us doubt ourselves, and hold us back. But we can take back control of our minds and have a more positive and hopeful view of life if we learn how to question and change negative thoughts.

Noticing negative thoughts is the first step to fighting them. It's hard to notice negative thoughts because they can become automatic and part of how we think. During this process, we need to teach our minds to be more aware and think about ourselves. We can start to see what causes negative thought patterns by watching our thoughts without judging them.

After we understand what negative thoughts are, we need to see if they are true and question their truthfulness. People often twist or blow up negative thoughts, which makes them seem true. This is where logic comes into play. We can ask ourselves questions like, "Is there real proof that this negative thought is true?" "Are there other ways to look at this or other explanations?" and "What would a friend or mentor you trust say about this idea?"

We can begin to diminish the influence of our negative thoughts by critically evaluating them. We can replace beliefs that are excessively extreme or unfounded with those that are more balanced and grounded in reality.

Changing how we think about things on purpose and looking for better, more positive ways to think about them is what reframing negative thoughts means. For example, instead of saying, "I always mess things up," we could say, "I've made mistakes in the past, but I'm always learning and growing." "Errors are chances to improve."

Another good way to deal with negative thoughts is to replace them with self-compassion. Instead of beating ourselves up for what we think are our failures or flaws, we can be understanding, kind, and helpful to ourselves. When we treat ourselves with the same kindness we would show a loved one, we can fight off negative thoughts and replace them with affirmations that make us feel stronger.

You also need to look for evidence that goes against the negative thoughts to challenge and change them. For example, when you start to think things like "I'm not good enough," you can remember times when you did well, got compliments from others, or had success. This practice helps to balance out negative thoughts about yourself and strengthen a more positive view of yourself.

Keep in mind that it takes time and practice to change negative thoughts. With consistent effort, we can change the way we think and become more positive over time. It won't happen overnight, but we can do it.

Challenging and reframing negative thoughts is a powerful way to build a positive and hopeful mindset. By being aware of our negative thoughts, checking to see if they are true, and replacing them with more balanced and positive ones, we can change how we feel about life. If we keep practicing and working at it, we can overcome the limits that negative thinking puts on us and adopt a mindset that helps us thrive and find joy in every part of our lives.

Learning to be grateful can change your life by bringing you joy, peace, and a new way of looking at things. It helps us change our focus from what we don't have or what is going wrong to what we do have and what is going well. It makes us grateful for the present and aware of the good things in our lives, no matter how big or small.

In addition to these planned activities, we also need to retrain our minds to be grateful all day. Notice the little things and events that usually go unnoticed. Take a break to enjoy a tasty meal, admire the beauty of nature, or enjoy the warmth of a hug. Being fully present and thankful for these moments adds gratitude to your daily life and makes you feel more fulfilled.

It can be hard to be grateful when things are hard or times are tough. But it's even more important to be grateful during these times. If we think of challenges as chances to grow, we can find hidden blessings and valuable lessons in them. Having a mindset that looks for things to be thankful for even when things are hard can help us build resilience and inner strength.

It's important to remember that being thankful every day takes work and commitment. Like any other habit, it takes time and effort to fully incorporate gratitude into our lives. Start with small, easy steps and gradually make your gratitude practice more frequent and deeper. As time goes on, you'll see that being thankful becomes a normal and important part of your daily life.

One way to enjoy the present moment is to engage your senses. Our senses connect us to the world around us, and by consciously tuning into them, we can make the present even more interesting. Take a moment to notice the bright colours of nature, the calming sounds of waves crashing or birds chirping, the soft touch of a loved one's hand, or the tempting smell of freshly brewed coffee. By really enjoying these sensory experiences, we can make the present moment more enjoyable and feel more connected to it.

We can see each moment in a new way and with an open mind when we cultivate a childlike sense of curiosity. We need to change the way we think so that we can enjoy the simple joys of everyday life and look for new experiences. If we approach life with a sense of curiosity, we can make our days more exciting and full of discovery by trying new hobbies, exploring new neighborhoods, or learning about new things.

Adding these habits to our daily lives can change how we feel about the present moment. We can have a lot of fun and learn a lot by using our senses, being curious, doing things that make us happy, connecting with others, and slowing down. There are endless ways to be happy in the present moment, and by fully accepting it, we can make our lives full of richness, thankfulness, and never-ending happiness.

It could be as simple as picking up a childhood hobby that has always made us happy, like painting, playing an instrument, or gardening. These activities can put us in a state of flow, where time seems to stop and we are completely in the moment. The creative process can be very therapeutic because it gives you a sense of peace and accomplishment.

For some people, exercise is the key to happiness. Exercise, whether it's sports, yoga, dancing, or something else, is good for our bodies and also releases endorphins, which are hormones that make us feel good. Moving around and feeling alive can have a big impact on our mood and how we see the world.

Being outside can also make you very happy and calm. Being in nature, whether it's hiking, walking along the beach, or just spending time in a park, is good for our health. The natural world is beautiful and peaceful, and it can help us feel grounded and thankful for the good things in life.

Being with family and friends or doing things with a group that we enjoy can make us feel like we belong and are happy. Having deep conversations, laughing with others, and making memories with them all make us feel more connected to them, which is a key part of being happy.

Also, doing things for other people and giving back to the community can make you feel very happy and like you have a purpose. By volunteering for a cause we believe in, we can help something bigger than ourselves. Helping others not only makes their lives better, but it also makes us feel grateful and fulfilled.

In the end, doing things that make us happy is a way to take care of ourselves and build a life that is true to who we are. We honour our uniqueness and put our own health first by making time for these activities on purpose. This creates a positive feedback loop: our happiness and optimism drive our actions, and our actions, in turn, make us happier and more optimistic.

We need to change the way we think so that we know that being optimistic is not just a passing feeling or a temporary state of mind; it is a way of life. When we choose to be optimistic, we choose to see the world through a lens of hope, strength, and opportunity. It is a conscious choice to focus on the possibilities in every situation and to face challenges with a positive and proactive attitude.

It's not enough to just do something once and forget about it; you have to work at it and be dedicated to keeping a positive attitude. By making positive habits a part of our daily lives, we can strengthen our minds, build our resilience, and find lasting happiness.

The way we talk to ourselves has a big impact on how we think, what we believe, and how we see the world. Talking to ourselves with kindness, support, and understanding all the time helps us believe in ourselves and feel good about ourselves. When we catch ourselves saying bad things about ourselves, we can change those thoughts into positive affirmations. This gives us power and helps us think more positively.

The people we hang out with and the places we go can have a big impact on how we see the world. When we choose to be around people who are positive and help us grow, we make an environment that helps us stay positive.

Consistent practice means staying committed to personal growth and self-improvement. It means being open to learning, changing, and accepting new points of view. When we always look for ways to grow, like reading, going to workshops, or asking mentors for help, we learn more and develop a mindset that is open to change and personal growth.

Letting go of old grudges and forgiving others has set me free. We have learned that holding onto grudges only makes us unhappy and stops us from being truly happy and at peace. By learning to forgive, we have let go of the burdens of the past. This has made room for healing, growth, and good relationships.

As we finish this chapter, let's celebrate how far we've come to change our minds for the better and become more positive and hopeful.

If we practice regularly, are determined, and believe in ourselves, we can say goodbye to our past and "Rewire Your Brain."

RESTRUCTURED
THINKING

Changing the way you think is not just a mental exercise; it can save the lives of people who have been through trauma, abuse, addiction, and the constant grip of racing, negative, and unwanted thoughts. For a lot of people, the mind is a place of pain instead of safety. Thoughts spiral out of control, memories come back, and self-esteem goes down. But the truth is that you can change your mind. It can be changed, healed, and made new. This isn't just a theory; it's something I've lived through and something I've seen happen to other people who were brave enough to believe that change was possible.

I remember the first time I realized that my thoughts weren't just random; they were patterns. I had a mental script that played on repeat after years of insecurities and low self-esteem. "You're not good enough." "You'll never be recognized." "You are stupid." "You will always be replaced."

These ideas didn't just pop into my head. They were planted by experiences, watered by fear, and made stronger by repeating them over and over again. I thought they were true because they sounded like things I already knew. But just because you know something doesn't mean it's true. It's just habit.

The Bible speaks to this in Lamentations 3:21–23: *"**Yet this I call to mind and therefore I have hope: Because of the Lord's great love we are not consumed, for his compassions never fail. They are new every morning; great is your faithfulness**."* That verse became a turning point for me. It reminded me that even when my thoughts felt consuming, I was not consumed. There was still hope. There was still compassion. And there was still the possibility of turning my life around.

Restructuring your thinking begins with awareness. You cannot change what you do not notice. For those with racing thoughts, this can feel impossible. The mind moves so fast, jumping from one fear to another, one regret to the next. But even in the chaos, there are moments of clarity. Moments when you can pause and say, "What am I thinking right now?" That pause is sacred. It's the doorway to change.

Negative thoughts often masquerade as facts. "I'm a failure." "No one loves me." "I'll never get better." These statements feel absolute, but they are interpretations. And interpretations can be challenged. One of the most powerful tools I learned was to ask myself, "Is this thought helpful?" Not "Is it true?"—because sometimes it feels true. But "Is it helpful?" That question shifted everything. It gave me permission to let go of thoughts that were hurting me, even if they felt familiar.

Romans 8:6 says, *"**The mind governed by the flesh is death, but the mind governed by the Spirit is life and peace**."* That verse speaks directly to the battle within. When our minds are governed by fear, shame, and addiction, we feel lifeless. But when we invite the Spirit to guide our thoughts, we begin to experience peace. Not perfect peace, not constant peace—but real peace. The kind that anchors us when the storm hits.

For those who have experienced trauma, restructuring your thinking also means rewriting your story. Trauma tells us we are powerless. It tells us the world is unsafe and that we are to blame. But those are lies. The truth is, trauma happened to you—it didn't define you. You are not the sum of your pain. You are the evidence of survival. And your thoughts can reflect that truth.

Philippians 4:6–7 offers a powerful promise: "***Do not be anxious about anything, but in every situation, by prayer and petition, with thanksgiving, present your requests to God. And the peace of God, which transcends all understanding, will guard your hearts and your minds in Christ Jesus.***" That peace is not passive—it's protective. It guards our minds. It stands at the gate and says, "Not every thought gets to enter."

Addiction complicates this process. Substance use often becomes a way to silence the mind. When thoughts are too loud, too painful, too overwhelming, drugs or alcohol offer escape. But escape is not healing. It's a detour that leads to deeper pain.

Restructuring your thinking in recovery means facing the thoughts you once ran from. It means learning to sit with discomfort and respond with compassion instead of avoidance.

One man I knew in recovery used to say, "My thoughts used to be my enemies. Now they're my teachers." He had spent years numbing his mind with cannabis and alcohol. But in sobriety, he began to listen. He began to ask, "What is this thought trying to tell me?" Sometimes it was fear. Sometimes it was grief. Sometimes it was a need for connection. By listening instead of running, he began to heal.

Psalm 139:23–24 became his daily prayer: "*Search me, God, and know my heart; test me and know my anxious thoughts. See if there is any offensive way in me, and lead me in the way everlasting.*"

That prayer is not just about confession—it's about invitation. It's saying, "God, help me see what I cannot see. Help me think differently."

Restructuring your thinking also involves creating new mental habits. Just as the mind can be trained to expect pain, it can be trained to expect peace. This takes practice. It takes repetition. It takes grace.

One of the most effective practices is gratitude. Not forced gratitude, not toxic positivity—but honest gratitude. "Today was hard, but I'm grateful I didn't give up." "I'm still hurting, but I'm grateful for this moment of calm." Gratitude rewires the brain. It shifts focus from lack to abundance, from fear to faith.

Another practice is visualization. Picture yourself thinking differently. Picture yourself responding to a trigger with calm instead of panic. Picture yourself speaking truth to a lie. Visualization activates the same neural pathways as actual behaviour. It prepares the mind for change. It makes healing feel possible.

I used to visualize myself walking through a storm with Jesus beside me. The wind was loud, the rain was heavy, but He was calm. He wasn't afraid. And because He wasn't afraid, I didn't have to be either. That image became my anchor. When my thoughts raced, I returned to it. When shame crept in, I returned to it. It reminded me that I was not alone.

Isaiah 26:3 says, "*You will keep in perfect peace those whose minds are steadfast, because they trust in you.*" That verse is a promise. Not of perfect circumstances, but of perfect peace. A peace that comes from trust. A peace that comes from steadiness. A peace that comes from restructuring our thoughts to align with truth.

Restructuring your thinking is cognitively reframing and restructuring your thoughts. These are not just therapeutic techniques—they are lifelines for those who have lived through trauma, abuse, addiction, and the relentless grip of racing, negative, and unwanted thoughts.

For many, the mind becomes a place of torment rather than refuge. Thoughts spiral, memories intrude, and self-worth erodes. But the truth is, the mind can be renewed. It can be reshaped, healed, and transformed. This isn't just a theory—it's a reality I've lived through, and one I've seen in others who dared to believe that change was possible.

I remember working with a young woman who had survived years of abuse. Her thoughts were filled with self-hatred and fear. She believed she was damaged beyond repair. But slowly, through therapy, prayer, and intentional thought work, she began to challenge those beliefs. She started writing down every negative thought and then writing a counter-thought rooted in truth. "I'm worthless" became "I am deeply loved." "I'll never heal" became "Healing is happening, even if I can't see it yet." Over time, her mind began to change. Not because she forced it, but because she fed it truth.

Cognitive restructuring also involves creating new mental habits. Just as the mind can be trained to expect pain, it can be trained to expect peace. This takes practice. It takes repetition. It takes grace.

For those in the midst of this journey, know this: your thoughts are not your destiny. They are not fixed. They are not final. They can be changed. They can be healed. They can be renewed. It will take time. It will take effort. It will take grace. But it is possible.

Start by noticing. Then by questioning. Then by replacing. Feed your mind truth. Feed it compassion. Feed it hope. Surround yourself with people who speak life. Create routines that support peace. And when you fall back into old patterns, don't shame yourself. Just begin again.

You are not broken. You are becoming. You are not lost. You are learning. You are not alone. You are loved.

Let your thoughts reflect that truth. Let your mind be a place of refuge. Let your thinking be a tool for healing. And let your journey be a testimony of transformation.

MASTER *Your* MIND

The mind is the most powerful gift we were created with, along with the heart, and if we don't use our minds correctly, it can be highly destructive. The thoughts that flow through our minds can either be a blessing or a curse.

The thoughts we entertain affect our perception and how we interpret information. We all struggle from time to time with our complex thinking patterns, however, with the help of divergent thinking, we can set our minds free.

We need to let our thoughts flow smoothly but should not allow them to rule us. Our thoughts can run wildly if we do not take control of them. Controlling our thoughts is like raising children. If we don't master parenting, our children will walk all over us. They will then bring shame and disrespect upon themselves and their families.

Similarly, lacking control over the mind will bring negative consequences. Unwanted thoughts that reside in our mind, will create unproductive and unhealthy thinking. Changing our thinking to dispel such thoughts will eventually allow us to control our behaviours.

Mastering the mind involves managing the thoughts that flow through the mind. It involves reprogramming our thinking. This takes skill and like any talent must be developed. Mastering the mind is like mastering a career or hobby, except the mind is with us twenty-four-seven.

Learning a language takes time, regardless of who we are and what culture or ethic background we are from. The speak a language with the perfect dialect takes a lot of effort and experience speaking.

Similarly, we can master our minds with the same principles. The more effort we give, the less stressful we will be in the process. Everything in life takes time to master like a language. The more we practice speaking it the more fluent it becomes.

When we master our thinking we can actually change our feelings which will enable a greater level of peace in our thought life. We can do two main things to take control of our minds; we can either replace our thinking with new thoughts or we can interrupt our thinking. Both require us to become more aware of impulsivity in our thoughts. When we master our minds, we will finally learn to control our thinking.

There are many thoughts that take up a lot of space in our brains. Like "squatters," who do not have permission to live in the location they chose. Some of our thoughts are there in our minds not because we have consciously given permission, but they came along as a result of past hurts.

The more they are fed with negativity they more controls they have and eventually they rule the mind just like a squatter who will take over land or a residence they reside in. In order to take charge, make sure you are the one consciously permitting these thoughts to stay in your mind, otherwise, dispel them.

There is usually a loose conglomeration of thoughts running through our minds that come from words that were spoken to us as children. It is often the case that these words take up space in our minds.

These are usually thoughts that have us comparing ourselves with others, believing that we are useless, feeling that we will never succeed, or constantly in a state of trying to fulfill other people's expectations of us.

The conglomeration of thoughts that come from rejection and betrayal which creates emotional pain should be discarded ceremoniously like putting an object that represents negativity in a box and burying or burning it. These are the thoughts that cripple us and instead of being a master over our minds, we become a slave to them.

We should never allow our thoughts to make us feel like we are in bondage or like we are a slave to fear and worry. Anger, frustration, emotional pain, and regrets grow when we live in bondage. A lack of motivation, low self-esteem, insecurity, anxiety, depression, passivity, and violent behaviours are all signs that we may be in bondage due to our thoughts.

Despite how much effect our thoughts can have on us, we are the masters of what we think. We need to stop ourselves from thinking negatively. Start by saying to yourself " I am in control." We can actually write it down or print on it paper "I am in control" and paste it in places where it is visible to remind ourselves we are in charge of ourselves. We should not be blaming others for our behaviours and actions.

Another behaviour we should avoid is beating up on ourselves. It is okay to admit our flaws and faults and move on. Don't allow thoughts of self-disappointment to stay in your brain. No one can change what has happened, however, we can problem-solve.

Therefore, looking for solutions instead of allowing negative thoughts to rule our minds should be our focus when things do not go the way we want them to. Sometimes we are our worst bullies. Don't allow your mind to bully you with negative thoughts.

Some unanswered questions that may help you that is usually asked. "What are some tricks and pointers to becoming masters of your minds?" "How do we get rid of the slave mentality?" "How do we take charge of our thinking?"

Most of us need to change our attitude toward ourselves and others at least at some point in our lives. We need to come to a place in life where we can conclude we don't have all the answers to all of life's problems and we cannot "fix" others who may have wronged us. Let that new positive attitude extend even to our enemies. When we start living in this fashion, we will grasp the basics of mastering our mind.

We should be alert to opportunities, realizing that opportunities may never come by again and take advantage of them when they are in your hands. We may fail, but that's a risk we will have to take. Each failure will draw us closer to the prize. Opportunities will expand our experience and develop our skill set.

We need to accept people for who they are instead of trying to change them to be us. We all do our own assessment of people we meet and make a conscious decision to engage with them or maintain a distance. Accepting the fact that we cannot change anyone but we can work with them is another skill we need in order to master the mind.

We can give suggestions and recommendations but cannot make someone become the person we want. A great deal of anxiety comes from feeling a lack of control when people do not behave how we want them to. People may even do things that can negatively influence us. Learning to accept others while being yourself and to let them make their own choices will have a positive impact on your relationship with them which in turn will positively impact your outlook.

When we take responsibility, we set a different paste in life. We create a blue print for others to follow. Regardless of what issues may arise as a result of our participation, we need learn to take responsibility. We could be 100% right or 100% wrong, we should take responsibility in finding a solution rather than blaming others.

This shows maturity but it is also a trick to allowing ourselves to learn that we are a master of our lives. So many of us live our lives more or less by ourselves and fail to include others. We need to ask ourselves why? Where did it stem from? We can socialize and engage with others and not allow the power of influence to affect us.

We can be in control of our mind, what we think of ourselves and others without allowing fear to control us. We were created to be among others to help with healthy stimulants, which assist with preventative factors that will affect our mental health long term.

We need to maintain a mind of a student. Some of us may give the impression that we know it all and that we have an answer for everything in life, yet our own lives are falling apart. It is only to compensate for self-perceived or actual incompetence. We can learn on a daily basis from other people around us.

We may learn minor things or get major revelations, but when we are willing to learn, we will always be one step closer to master what we are learning. Assuming the role of a student allows for new thoughts to replace discarded thoughts as we stay in control of what we allow into our minds.

We also need to maintain a mind of a teacher. One thing observed from teaching is that it forces you to learn. When time is spent preparing a lesson, knowledge is gained. And, when we teach, experience and skills are sharpened.

Being a teacher sometimes forces us to take control of what we are saying and how we are saying it to ensure that others receive our message effectively. Find out how we can speak into the lives of others even if it's our love ones. The concept of centering our thoughts around communicating a theme will help us in taking control of our thought life.

When the brain is "infected," things can go awry, and the brain no longer serves its purpose efficiently. Symptoms of thought disorders will result as the brain can no longer "carry a conversation" that is sensible.

Our brain is a miracle how it function as it holds more information than we could ever imagine. It houses resources we can tap into in the future in an orderly fashion which enables us to perform various impressive tasks.

Think of the first time you tried riding a bike. Your brain needed to recall many thoughts in order to keep the bike upright, and it does not matter how many years later you will still know how to ride a bike.

We can become great servants to our minds if we fail to become masters over it. We may find ourselves feeling we cannot control what we think, do or say, but it is possible with proper discipline. Spend time concentrating and thinking through your thoughts before acting, forming opinions, or communicating opinions. We need to learn how to filter our thoughts if we want to master them.

Mastering our minds draws us closer to the destinies assigned to us. We need to come to a place where we can master our minds, otherwise we will never be at peace with ourselves. We need to control what goes into our mind.

If it's not good for you, cut it out otherwise it will become like cancer and can destroy you. Our thoughts based on the five sensory systems which are the precursors to our emotions and the actions we take.

Mastering our minds will help us to manage the thoughts that plays in our minds, affecting how we feel, what we do, and what comes out of our mouths.

We should never ignore our "gut feeling." Many times before we feed our thought, we have a "gut feeling" that we ignore. If you don't feel good about something, don't pursue it. Sometimes it could be something simple like going over to visit a friend.

You are aware your friend is into things you have been working on in your personal life (drinking alcohol, using street drugs, pornography, video games, and so on). You are aware every time you visit your friend, you end up doing things you should not do. If you have a "gut feeling", put a peace to the warning thoughts by exploring all the things that can go wrong. Be alert and aware. Many of us usually gets trapped into deciding against our "gut feeling," and have regrets.

Some of the choices we make triggers our past creating more psychological issues affecting our mental health. When we develop unhealthy coping strategies, they can become our default mode to cope when under stress. The mind will lead you to fall into old habits. However when we master our mind, we can chose alternatives that are new which we can set as new default modes.

A healthy neuropathways as an example would be someone who used to use alcohol to cope. The individual may choose to drink club soda with a lime or lemon to avoid drinking alcohol especially at family events. It is a parallelism to the old pathway.

Some individuals may choose to set themselves to have one drink which is monitored by their spouse or family member as a healthy way to drink alcohol, which is another parallelism. Street drugs, misuse of prescription medications, gambling, and other addictions are considered unhealthy copying strategies which need new healthy parallelism to cope with life's stressors.

Another interesting thought is learning to say 'No.' The desire to say "no" when we have all intentions to say "yes". If we yield ourselves to what is being asked that is not in our favour, it may lead us to fall into a trap that stimulates negative thoughts.

Learning to say "no" is okay and that is one thought we should have flowing in our minds. Some people say yes all the time working all types of extra shifts, helping others move, going to different functions when asked, making donations to everyone who asks, buying items when on sale, buying from door-to-door sellers, going to their friend's sports games, and so on.

Learning to say no will help to stay focused on what is most important. Learning to prioritize what is most important will help to become more progressive in life. And this will be another perfect example of mastering the mind, when not driven by impulsivity.

We need to control our assumptions as they can recondition the mind to carry the wrong message. Controlling our thoughts from the assumption of what is being texted, emailed, or on the phone. So many time we make a presumption as to what we read, not knowing the full story or the content of what is being written.

Some people may have difficulty expressing themselves over the phone, in texting, and emailing. Developing a thought which is usually negative about a phone call, a text, or an email will play in your mind like a movie.

The best is face-to-face or making sure you understand the person you are communicating with before you allow your thought to create a conclusion. It's easy to create thoughts, but they can be very challenging to get rid of.

We need to control planting negative thoughts since they are like weeds that can take over our mind from the fruitfulness of being or staying positive. How many of us try to convince others to like what we like, or steer a conversation for others to adapt or engage in? We then become frustrated when the conversation is not going the way we assumed in our minds.

We try to make our only conclusion about what the other person's reaction is, what they may say, their mood, how they dress, and their non-verbal language. We try to control others by how we carry on a conversation and not monitoring that we are the dominant ones in the conversation.

We speak words to stir the person's emotion or awaken their thoughts, especially if we know some of their weakness or what they have an interest in. We try to live like sales' people, sharing our thoughts to get others to share and then plant our thought seeds into their minds.

Some of us hide our insecurity by speaking negatively about everyone. We have nothing good to say and allow our thoughts that are being created to be negative.

Everyone we speak with, we speak to them about someone else. We only see negative attributes and nothing positive comes out of our month. We may not see it and the people we associate with it would not say anything since they want to hear the gossip.

Although they are aware that the person who is speaking negatively is also speaking negatively about them behind their back, they continue to feed the person's ego. Negativity feeds on your life and will draw joy from your heart. It's better to walk away and refocus your thoughts on something healthy for the mind.

We have the ability to be resilient. Which means we can train our minds to stay positive, even as we develop our dreams, set goals for our lives, work on plans, and stay on track.

We are in control of our thoughts and can do whatever we put our mind to do. We have more control over our thoughts than we may give ourselves credit for. We need to utilize the power of our thought to change the world around us.

With that being said, we need to manage our impulsivity in making decisions, responding to conversations, buying things and voicing our opinions especially when we were not asked to share it.

Some of us can be impulsive and have an automatic reaction when others speak to us. It's like if someone were to attempt to hit us, we block ourselves from being hurt. We have an automatic reaction in which at times we can say things that can be offensive toward others and bring emotional harm to ourselves.

We need to learn how to manage these automatic thoughts and allow our emotional skills to be a thicker than tomato skin. We all need to consider how we should respond to others if they enforce their thoughts on us. What would be your reaction and how would you psychologically deal with it?

Some of us can be defensive with what we say, harsh, cold, emotionless, and unrealistic. We need to consider what we give out, others will react the same and lash back. We all need to learn to be realistic in how we behave with what we say.

We should ask ourselves " is it logical," "are we watching the tone of our voices," "are we being "black and white" in our conversation, not willing to listen to those who are in the grey?" "Are we being mindful that others may have value in what they are saying as much as what we say?"

We need to learn how to be our defense lawyer and cross-exam ourselves to ensure that we are accommodating others as much as we want others to accommodate us.

Learning the process of how we think and what we may need to change to associate with others is important, otherwise, we may live with a delusion that others want to be in our presence when in reality they are afraid of telling us the truth of how they feel about us.

We need to learn to recognize our limitations and speak to others with an understanding that we can make mistakes and is opened for corrections. We need to acknowledge that others have tons of value to add to the conversation.

We will carry a long conversation without making others feel they are walking on eggshells. This is a good sign that we are mastering our minds and taking control of our thoughts.

We need to learn that some things we think, we need to put on the shelf, especially if becomes an obstacle in our relationships with others. Learning that our mind can think faster than we can comprehend and the need not to act on what we think at times is healthy.

Mastering the mind gives us that power to be in control, especially when we can remind ourselves that we don't have to give an answer to every question, we don't have to react to every emotion from others, we don't have to be impulsive, and that time is our best friend.

We can always give an answer when the dust settles, and we give ourselves some time to process a conversation that may be tense. Mastering the mind is being able to weed out anything that may come across harmful, demanding, questioning, parenting and objective.

THE *Three* MINDS

Philosophers, psychologists, and scientists have been interested in how strong and complex the human mind is for hundreds of years. Our minds combine our thoughts, feelings, and choices, which change how we see the world and the direction our lives go.

We need to know how the emotional, logical, and wise parts of our minds work together. We need to figure out what makes each mind different and how they can help us learn about ourselves and the world around us.

Talking to our own minds isn't always easy. Sometimes our thoughts, feelings, and wants can pull us in different directions, which can lead to problems and fights within ourselves. We can negotiate in our own minds in a way that works and brings together our emotional, rational, and wise minds. This means finding things we all agree on, figuring out what we really want and value, and bringing all three minds together.

The first mind is the emotional mind, which makes up our mental landscape. This is where our wants, needs, and feelings come from. Our emotional brains have a big effect on how we see, feel, think, act, and make decisions every day. It can make us less clear-headed or lead us in the wrong direction, which can change how we make decisions.

Sometimes it can give us useful information and help us get the best results. Our emotional minds are like tomatoes in that they have thin skin and can feel everything, even things that aren't said. We make choices and come up with new plans based on how we feel instead of thinking about the facts and reasons that led us to that thought or action. This can be a problem. Tomatoes are usually sweet and juicy, but they can be hurt easily.

Our feelings can affect other people, and other people's feelings can change how we make decisions. When people around us are feeling strongly, it can change how we feel and what we decide to do. If a lot of people in a group are excited about a certain choice, we might be more likely to go along with what everyone else is doing and make choices based on how everyone else is feeling. We should be aware of this effect and think about whether the choices we make are in line with what we want and what we believe.

Our feelings can make us biased when we make choices. This means that how we feel might make us choose one option or point of view over another. For instance, when we're scared or nervous, we might choose the safest or most familiar option, even if it's not the best one. But feeling good can also make people too confident and willing to take risks. Knowing about these biases can help us make better choices and understand things from other people's points of view.

If you don't take care of your emotional mind, maintain emotional regulation and think about the big picture in life, it can hurt for a long time. We can't heal if we keep thinking about how bad the wounds make us feel.

When our emotional mind is in charge, it's easy to react without thinking about what is being said. Our primary thought is expressed, whereas our secondary thought comprises our processed thoughts.

Emotional mind regulation is the ability to handle and control our feelings in a good way. When we're really angry or sad, it can be hard to think clearly, which can make us do things that don't make sense or that we don't want to do.

We can make better choices if we are emotionally smart and know ourselves. This helps us understand and control our feelings better. It's easy to think that everyone is against us when they don't agree with us. We think of people as friends when they agree with us. But that could change at any time.

It can be hard to learn how to agree to disagree because we don't always know what it means. We need to know that our feelings can be both good and bad at the same time. It can be hard to learn how to grow the good emotional mind, but it is possible.

Our emotional mind can change how we think and what we do when we have to make a choice. We can make choices that don't make sense or act on impulse when we're scared, angry, or excited. But emotions can also tell us a lot about what we like, what we want, and what we value. We should be aware of and understand our feelings, but we shouldn't let them take over our minds.

Understanding how feelings affect decisions is an important step toward finding a balance between the emotional and rational mind. We can make better choices if we learn more about ourselves, how to control our feelings, and how to be smart with our feelings. We can use the wisdom of the wise mind to make choices that are good for us and in line with our values when we use both our minds and our hearts.

When we make decisions, we need to remember that logic and reason are just as important as our feelings. The rational mind which is the second mind is the part of the mind that handles facts, logical thinking, objective analysis, and critical reasoning. We can use this mind to look at information, think about the pros and cons, and make smart decisions. It can also help us deal with the strong emotions that can take over at times.

The emotional mind and the rational mind are both present in Scripture, often in tension, yet designed to work together in wisdom and faith. The emotional mind feels deeply—joy, sorrow, anger, compassion—while the rational mind discerns, plans, and judges rightly. Together, they reflect the fullness of human experience and the image of God.

In Proverbs 4:23, we are told, *"Above all else, guard your heart, for everything you do flows from it."* The heart in biblical language often represents the emotional center. It is the seat of desire, affection, and motivation.

Emotions are not dismissed in Scripture; they are acknowledged as powerful forces that shape behaviour. Yet they must be guarded—not suppressed, but guided.

Jeremiah 17:9 warns, *"The heart is deceitful above all things and beyond cure. Who can understand it?"* This verse reminds us that emotions, while real and valid, can mislead. The emotional mind can be swayed by fear, pride, or pain. That is why the rational mind, shaped by truth and discernment, is essential. Rational renewal is not cold logic—it is spiritual clarity.

Jesus Himself demonstrates the balance. In John 11:35, He weeps at Lazarus's tomb. His emotional response is full and human. Yet moments later, He raises Lazarus from the dead, acting with divine authority and purpose. His emotions do not hinder His mission—they deepen it. The emotional mind connects us to others; the rational mind helps us act wisely.

Ecclesiastes 3:4 says there is "*a time to weep and a time to laugh, a time to mourn and a time to dance.*" This rhythm affirms that emotions have their place. They are not weaknesses but seasons. The rational mind discerns the time; the emotional mind enters it fully. Wisdom is knowing when to feel and when to act.

In Luke 10:27, Jesus affirms the greatest commandment: "*Love the Lord your God with all your heart and with all your soul and with all your strength and with all your mind.*" This verse integrates both emotional and rational faculties. Love is not just a feeling—it is a decision, a strength, and a thought. The whole person is called into relationship with God.

Paul writes in Philippians 4:7 that "*the peace of God, which transcends all understanding, will guard your hearts and your minds in Christ Jesus.*" Peace is both emotional and rational. It calms the heart and steadies the mind. It is not the absence of thought or feeling, but the harmony of both under God's care.

In 2 Timothy 1:7, Paul reminds us that "*God gave us a spirit not of fear but of power and love and self-control.*" Fear is an emotional response, but self-control is a rational discipline. The Spirit empowers both. Love fuels the emotional mind; self-control guides the rational mind. Together, they reflect spiritual maturity.

The Psalms are full of emotional expression—grief, joy, anger, longing. David cries out in Psalm 42:11, "*Why, my soul, are you downcast? Why so disturbed within me? Put your hope in God.*" Here, the emotional mind is honest, and the rational mind responds with hope. The psalmist does not deny his feelings; he speaks truth to them.

In James 1:19, we are instructed to be *"quick to listen, slow to speak and slow to become angry."* This is a call to regulate emotion through reason. Anger is not condemned, but it is cautioned. Listening is a rational act that tempers emotional reaction. Wisdom is found in the pause between feeling and response.

The emotional mind and the rational mind are not enemies. They are companions in the journey of faith. Scripture does not elevate one above the other—it calls both to be surrendered to God. The emotional mind brings depth; the rational mind brings direction. Together, they form a heart and mind that are wise, compassionate, and ready to follow the Spirit.

We need to find a balance between our emotions and our reason to make the best decisions and get the best results. It's important to find the right balance between your logical and emotional mind when you make decisions. Both are important.

You need a reasonable mind to think critically, figure things out, and weigh the pros and cons of different choices. But when the reasonable mind is in charge of making choices, it can make people less concerned about how their choices affect other people. A lot of men may think this way because they don't want to show how they feel, which is a sign of weakness.

A cantaloupe is a good example of a reasonable mind: it's sweet on the inside but hard on the outside. This mind made it hard for someone to connect with and understand other people. They may not be sure of themselves or feel safe, so keeping their feelings to themselves makes them feel safe.

But to get the best results, you usually need to find a good balance between how you feel and how you think. If you can get these two minds to work together, you can make better and more nuanced choices.

To better understand tough situations and come up with the best answers, we need to find a balance between our feelings and our logic.

Using your rational mind to make good choices is very important. We need to use logic to make smart choices, even though our feelings can help us make decisions and give us useful information. We can look at things objectively, think about the facts and evidence that matter, and figure out what might happen if we choose a certain path when we use our reasonable mind.

The logical mind tells us to gather and look at the relevant information before making a choice. We can use our critical thinking skills to check if the sources are honest and reliable, look for biases, and weigh the evidence. We can make good choices when we base them on facts and objective data.

A rational mind helps us see how our choices affect other things. We can think about how each choice will affect us and other people in the long run if we know what could happen if we make different choices. This analysis helps us pick things that fit with what we want and believe.

The rational mind helps us figure out how likely and dangerous different things are. By looking at the information we have and weighing the pros and cons of each, we can make educated guesses about how likely different scenarios are. This evaluation helps us make better choices by weighing the possible benefits against the risks.

Cognitive biases are natural tendencies that can cause us to make choices that don't make sense. We can see these biases and deal with them by using our common sense. We can use logic to figure out when cognitive biases like confirmation bias (favouring information that supports what we already believe) or anchoring bias (putting too much weight on initial information) might be affecting how we think. If we know about these biases and work to fight them, we can make better choices.

Inductive reasoning starts with specific observations and ends with general principles. Deductive reasoning, on the other hand, starts with general principles and ends with specific outcomes. You can use either type of reasoning to make decisions.

We can use deductive reasoning to figure out what makes sense based on what we already know and the rules we already follow. Inductive reasoning helps us think of new things and make smart guesses. These kinds of reasoning help us organize our thoughts and look at things from different points of view.

Fairness means hearing what other people have to say. We can make better choices when we listen to what other people have to say and ask for their opinions. Rationality enables us to assess the information we receive objectively, ascertain its relevance, and incorporate it into our decision-making process.

We can make better choices if we understand how important the rational mind is and how to balance it with the emotional mind. We can find a middle ground between the two by accepting the rational, emotional, and wise minds. This means thinking about both the facts and how they make us feel. In the end, this mix leads to choices that make sense and are in line with our values, feelings, and long-term goals.

The wise mind is the third mind which is a mix of the emotional and the rational minds. It's a way of making choices that uses both logic and feelings. We need to use our gut feelings, listen to the voice of the Holy Spirit inner wisdom, and a deeper understanding of ourselves and the situation to be smart. When we use our wise mind, we make decisions that are in line with our values, think about how our choices will affect us and others, and think about how they will affect us in the long run.

A wise mind is one that has a lot of knowledge, intuition, and insight. It's not just the logical and emotional minds. The wise mind uses what we learn from our experiences, the mix of our emotional and rational minds, and a deep understanding of who we are. We will talk about how having a wise mind can help us make better choices and get results that are in line with our long-term health, values, and goals.

It's good to know about these different parts of the mind because it helps us figure out what they do well and what they don't do well. We can learn more about ourselves and make better choices if we understand how our thoughts and feelings affect our decisions.

The wise mind is a key part of making decisions because it works with the parts of the mind that are logical and rational. We need to use both our emotional and rational minds, but intuition can help us see things in a new way that can lead to new ideas and good results. You could say that this is the smart mind. We can grow the wise mind by balancing and combining our emotional and logical minds.

You use your wise mind to make decisions when you trust your gut and don't think only about what you know. Then we can make good choices for the future by doing what is best for us and others.

A smart person knows things deeply and instinctively, without having to think about them. It means getting information and patterns that the conscious mind can't always see.

Intuitive insights frequently emerge as abrupt "aha" moments, intensified emotions, or a feeling of certainty. Intuition is hard to define and measure, but it can help people decide what to do.

The wise mind is a "gut" feeling that comes from deep inside us. You could say we have a "knowing" or a strong gut feeling about what is right and wrong. These feelings are often connected to how our bodies respond, like when our hearts race or our stomachs tighten. When we trust our gut feelings, we listen to these physical sensations and use them to help us decide what to do.

According to Scriptures, one that reveres God, listens deeply, discerns truth, and walks humbly. It is not merely intellectual but spiritual—rooted in the fear of the Lord and shaped by divine insight.

Proverbs 9:10 declares, *"The fear of the Lord is the beginning of wisdom, and knowledge of the Holy One is understanding."* This reverence is the foundation of all wise thinking, reminding us that wisdom begins not with self-confidence but with surrender.

The wise mind is slow to speak and quick to listen. Proverbs 18:13 warns, *"To answer before listening—that is folly and shame."* Wisdom listens first, not only to people but to God. It pauses, reflects, and waits for clarity.

James 1:5 encourages us to ask for wisdom, promising that God gives generously to those who seek it. This means wisdom is not a possession but a gift—one that grows through prayer, patience, and openness.

A wise mind is not shaped by trends or pressure but by transformation. It is renewed through Scripture, through reflection, and through the Spirit's guidance. This renewal allows us to discern what is good, pleasing, and perfect in God's will.

James 3:17 describes wisdom as *"pure, peace-loving, considerate, submissive, full of mercy and good fruit, impartial and sincere."* These qualities show that wisdom is relational. It is not harsh or arrogant but gentle and fair. A wise mind does not dominate—it serves. It does not manipulate—it understands. It does not rush—it waits.

Ecclesiastes 7:10 cautions, *"Do not say, 'Why were the old days better than these?' For it is not wise to ask such questions."*

Wisdom does not cling to nostalgia or resist change. It embraces the present and remains open to growth. A wise mind is flexible, able to adapt without losing its anchor in truth.

Jesus models the wise mind throughout His ministry. In Luke 13, when He heals a woman on the Sabbath, He challenges rigid thinking by asking, *"Shouldn't this woman, a daughter of Abraham, whom Satan has kept bound for eighteen long years, be set free on the Sabbath day?"* His question reframes tradition through compassion. Wisdom, in this moment, is not about rule-keeping but about restoration.

Paul's words in 2 Timothy 2:7 invite reflection: *"Think about what I am saying, for the Lord will give you insight into all this."* A wise mind is not hasty. It thinks again. It revisits ideas and allows the Spirit to illuminate them over time. Insight is not always immediate—it unfolds.

In Proverbs 2:6 we read, *"For the Lord gives wisdom; from His mouth come knowledge and understanding."* This verse reminds us that wisdom is divine in origin. It is not earned by intellect but received through relationship. The wise mind is a listening mind, a discerning mind, a mind that seeks God above all.

The wise mind is not a substitute for reason and logic; rather, it is an enhancement of them. When you have to choose, you should think about both what you want and what makes sense. Rationality gives us a structured and analytical way of thinking, while the wise mind can give us a bigger picture that includes subtle cues and unspoken understanding. Putting the two together helps us make better choices that are based on more information.

You need to know yourself and practice being present to get a wise mind. We can learn more about how our intuition works by paying more attention to our thoughts, feelings, and what our bodies are doing. Also, remembering times when our wise mind was right and things that have happened in the past can help us trust our "gut" feelings.

We need to learn how to think wisely if we want to use the power of our minds. It helps us deal with new things, solve hard problems, and come up with new ideas. To get better at solving problems, we need to be open to different points of view, question what we think we know, and accept that we don't know everything.

You need to learn how to think wisely if you want to solve problems better. This lets you change how you think and act in different situations. You need to know what the wise mind is to get better at this. It means being able to switch between your emotional and rational mind when things change. This includes things like feelings, attention, perception, facts, logic, rationalizations, and ways to solve problems.

Having a growth mindset is a good way to make the wise mind stronger. You can look at problems in a more open and flexible way if you believe that you can get smarter and better at things by working hard and learning. When you have a growth mindset, you look for challenges and see failures as chances to learn and get better. This helps you change and come up with new ideas.

It's good for growing the wise mind to do things that are hard for your mind. You have to think critically, look at things from different points of view, and change your plan based on what you learn when you do puzzles, brainteasers, strategy games, and other tasks that are hard for your brain. These things help your brain learn to be more flexible and find new ways to solve problems.

When you accept the unknown, you can look into new options and think of other ways to solve problems. If you know that not all problems have easy answers and that there can be more than one way to solve a problem, you can think more freely and come up with new ways to do things.

You also need to question what you believe and what you think is true in order to grow a wise mind. When you question your own ideas, you can make room for new ones. This new way of thinking can help you come up with new and more creative ways to solve problems and find solutions that you might not have thought of before.

Divergent thinking is the process of coming up with a lot of different ways to fix a problem. You can get a wise mind and come up with a lot of different ideas by doing creative things or brainstorming exercises that make you think outside the box. This method helps people who are stuck in their ways and makes it easier for them to come up with new ideas for how to solve problems.

When we have to make a choice, we often have to talk to all three of our minds at once: our emotional mind, our rational mind, and our wise mind. These three parts of the mind show how different people and ideas can change what we do and what we choose. To make smart and well-rounded choices when you negotiate with yourself, you need to find a balance between these three things.

Before you can start negotiating with yourself, you need to learn more about who you are. This means being aware of and accepting your feelings, thoughts, and biases that could change how you make choices. You can better deal with the conflicting thoughts and feelings that come up when you have to make a choice if you know how your mind works.

You need to work on how well you understand and control your feelings if you want to be able to negotiate well with yourself. Emotional intelligence is the ability to know, understand, and control your own feelings and those of other people. You can handle strong feelings like anger or fear and make decisions that aren't just based on how you feel by improving your emotional intelligence.

It's also important to use your smart mind when you choose. It's important to use logic and reason, but our wise mind can help us see things in a way that goes beyond just thinking about them. A wise mind often comes from taking in information without thinking about it, and it can give you a full picture of what's going on. You can get to a deeper level of wisdom and make better choices by listening to your wise mind and using your rational mind.

You can get better at switching between your wise, emotional, and rational minds with practice. It needs improved emotional intelligence, cognitive flexibility, and mindfulness. The main goal is to find peace and balance in these mental areas so that we can make decisions that are both emotionally and logically sound.

In short, learning more about how the mind works and what it can do can help us make better decisions and feel better overall. In this chapter, we looked at how the emotional mind, the rational mind, and the wise mind all work together in strange ways. By breaking these parts down, we have learned a lot about how our thoughts, feelings, and reasoning affect the choices we make and the things we do.

You need to practice, be patient, and be nice to yourself if you want to learn how to negotiate with your own mind. We can choose to change our focus and use the wisdom of the wise mind when we know which part of our mind is in charge of making decisions: our emotional mind or our rational mind. This negotiation helps us find balance and peace within ourselves, which helps us make better choices.

THE POWER *Of*
RESILIENCY

Problems, setbacks, and surprises are things we have to deal with in life that can make us feel like we don't have control over our lives. But we are very good at getting through tough times and coming out stronger than before. Being resilient means being able to handle both the good and bad times in life with strength and grace.

Resiliency is not just a reaction to hardship—it's a rhythm of grace and grit that God has woven into our design. We are created with natural resiliency: the ability to adapt, endure, and recover. But we are also gifted with spiritual resiliency, which allows us to rise not just with strength, but with purpose. I've seen both in my life—sometimes in quiet moments of perseverance, sometimes in dramatic pivots that only faith could explain.

When I was refining my book, I hit a wall. The message was clear in my heart, but the words felt tangled. I spent hours editing, rewriting, praying. My natural resiliency helped me stay focused, analyze structure, and push through fatigue. But spiritual resiliency reminded me why I was writing in the first place. I leaned into Romans 8:28: *"And we know that in all things God works for the good of those who love Him."* That verse gave me peace. Even the struggle was part of the story.

There was a time in my life when everything felt like it was breaking at once—emotionally, financially, spiritually. I remember it vividly. We were missionaries in Croatia, pouring our hearts into the work, when my friend Tihomir was killed. That moment shattered something in me. He wasn't just a friend—he was a brother in the Lord, someone who shared the same fire for the gospel, the same love for people. I remember the numbness, the disbelief. I remember asking God, "Why him? Why now?" And yet, even in that grief, something deeper stirred. I didn't collapse. I wept, yes. I mourned. But I also kept going. That was spiritual resiliency—God holding me when I couldn't hold myself.

I leaned into Psalm 34:18: *"The Lord is close to the broken-hearted and saves those who are crushed in spirit."* I felt that closeness. Not in a loud, miraculous way, but in the quiet strength that helped me get up each day and keep serving.

I still had people to care for, messages to deliver, and a family to lead. My natural resiliency kicked in too—the part of me that could organize meals, comfort others, and keep the mission moving. But it was spiritual resiliency that helped me forgive, that helped me believe Tihomir's death wasn't the end of his story.

Then there was the season when we were back home, raising seven children with barely enough to get by. We were broke. I mean, really broke. There were days when I didn't know how we'd pay for groceries, let alone tuition. And yet, I went back to school. It sounds crazy when I say it out loud—seven kids, no money, and I'm studying again. But I knew it was what I had to do. Natural resiliency helped me manage the chaos—packing lunches, helping with homework, studying late into the night while the house was finally quiet. I was tired, but I kept going.

What kept me from giving up was something deeper. Spiritual resiliency reminded me that God had called me to this. That He was in the details. Philippians 4:19 became my anthem: ***"And my God will meet all your needs according to the riches of His glory in Christ Jesus."*** I clung to that promise. And somehow, the needs were met.

Not always in the way I expected, but always in time. A gift here, a scholarship there, a door opening just when I thought it was all closing.

There were moments when I felt like I was walking on water—completely dependent on God to keep me from sinking. And there were moments when I felt like Peter, looking at the waves and starting to go under. But every time, Jesus reached out His hand. That's spiritual resiliency. It's not the absence of fear or fatigue—it's the presence of faith in the middle of it.

I've learned that resilience isn't about being strong all the time. It's about being willing. Willing to keep showing up. Willing to trust again. Willing to believe that God is still writing the story, even when the page I'm on feels like a mess. I've lived that. I've walked through grief, through scarcity, through uncertainty. And I've seen how God uses both the natural strength He built into us and the supernatural strength He offers us to carry us through.

So when I talk about resilience, I'm not speaking from theory. I'm speaking from the trenches. From the nights I cried out to God. From the mornings I got up anyway. From the moments I chose to believe that love was stronger than loss, that calling was stronger than circumstance, and that grace was always enough.

Joseph's story in Genesis is one I return to often. Betrayed by his brothers, sold into slavery, falsely imprisoned—his natural resiliency is remarkable. He interprets dreams, manages resources, and eventually becomes ruler of Egypt. But his spiritual resiliency is what transforms the narrative. When his brothers return, he says, *"You meant evil against me, but God meant it for good"* (Genesis 50:20). That perspective doesn't come from logic alone—it comes from grace. Joseph doesn't just survive; he redeems.

Jesus shows us the deepest form of spiritual resiliency. In the Garden of Gethsemane, He says, *"My soul is overwhelmed with sorrow to the point of death"* (Matthew 26:38). He feels the weight of suffering, yet He prays, *"Not my will, but Yours be done."* That surrender is not weakness—it's strength. It's the kind of resilience that transforms pain into purpose.

I've seen this in my own spiritual walk. When I've felt spiritually dry or emotionally stretched, I've returned to Psalm 42:11: *"Why, my soul, are you downcast? Why so disturbed within me? Put your hope in God."* That verse doesn't deny emotion—it speaks truth to it. It's a reminder that hope is a choice, and resilience is a practice.

Natural resiliency helps me manage the day-to-day: deadlines, transitions, responsibilities. It's the part of me that can plan, pivot, and persist. But spiritual resiliency helps me interpret those experiences through the lens of grace. It's what allows me to forgive, to hope, and to love even when things are uncertain.

In 2 Corinthians 12:9, Paul writes, *"My grace is sufficient for you, for My power is made perfect in weakness."* That verse has carried me through seasons of exhaustion. It reminds me that resilience isn't about being invincible—it's about being surrendered. When I've felt stretched thin, I've leaned into grace, and found strength I didn't know I had.

There was a time when I was helping someone navigate a crisis of faith. They were questioning everything—God's goodness, their own worth, the meaning of suffering. I didn't try to fix it. I shared my own story, my own doubts, and the verses that had held me together. Lamentations 3:22–23 came to mind: "*Because of the Lord's great love we are not consumed, for His compassions never fail. They are new every morning; great is Your faithfulness.*" That truth doesn't erase pain—it anchors us in it.

Resilience is not perfection—it's persistence. It's the ability to bend without breaking, to feel deeply without losing direction, and to rise again with new strength. We are built with natural tools—intellect, emotion, adaptability. But we are also equipped with spiritual gifts— faith, hope, love. When we tap into both, we become not just survivors, but healers, leaders, and creators.

And when we do, we reflect the heart of Christ—who endured suffering, embraced humanity, and rose again with power. Hebrews 12:2 says, "*For the joy set before Him, He endured the cross, scorning its shame, and sat down at the right hand of the throne of God.*" That joy—that vision beyond pain—is what spiritual resiliency gives us. It's the strength to keep going, not because we're strong, but because we're held.

That's the kind of resilience I want to live by. The kind that weaves together the natural and the spiritual, the practical and the profound. The kind that says, "I've been through the fire, but I'm still here. And I'm still growing."

It's not enough to just get back up; you have to get back up stronger. We talk about how to handle problems and make them opportunities for growth and improvement. By learning from our mistakes and accepting the lessons they teach us, we can become more resilient and stronger than ever.

We can now look into different strategies and techniques that we can use every day. By putting together a resilience toolkit, we give ourselves the tools we need to deal with life's problems head-on and win. And this means that failing can help you succeed. We need to learn how to change our minds about failure and use it to help us grow and come up with new ideas.

In a world that is always changing and full of surprises, being able to bounce back is very important. We accept that things can be uncertain and change, and we see these things as ways to help us grow as individuals and as a group. By changing how we see things and accepting the unknown, we can build a strong mindset that helps us adapt and do well even when things are uncertain.

Resilience isn't just about the person; it's also about how we treat other people. That's why we need to focus on relationships. You need to know how to handle disagreements and issues in relationships. We talk about how important resilience is for making strong connections that can handle hard times and last a long time.

By learning about and using the power of resilience, we give ourselves the strength to deal with life's problems, turn failures into opportunities, and build a resilience that helps us thrive in a world that is always changing.

When things get hard, resiliency is the ability to bounce back, get better, and change (Masten, A. S., 2018). It is the ability to handle and move on from tough times in life, like losing a job, going through trauma, or dealing with stress. Being strong doesn't mean staying away from or getting rid of problems. Instead, it means figuring out how to deal with them and move on.

It is important to be resilient because life is full of surprises and everyone has hard times. Resilience helps us handle big problems in life and everyday stress, keep our mental health in check, and do well even when things are hard. It keeps our minds and emotions stable, which helps us learn, adapt, and grow from hard times.

We are more likely to see problems as temporary and fixable when we are strong. We are more persistent, determined, and positive, which helps us stay focused on our goals even when things get hard. People who are resilient are better at handling problems, keeping their feelings in check, and finding ways to deal with stress and stay mentally healthy.

Being resilient is a big part of becoming a better person and growing as a person. It encourages us to step outside of our comfort zones, take risks, and try new things. We get better at things, feel more sure of ourselves, and know what we're doing when we face and beat challenges. Resilience helps us have a growth mindset, which means we learn from our mistakes, change our plans, and keep getting better.

Resilience is good for our health and for our relationships, communities, and society as a whole. When things get tough, strong people can help and support others, which helps create strong social networks and a sense of collective strength. By showing that failures are not the end, but rather chances to grow and change, they inspire and motivate others.

Resilience is not only a psychological trait; it is fundamentally rooted in neuroscience. Understanding how the brain helps us be strong can help us understand why some people are better at handling problems and getting back on track after a setback.

Neuroplasticity is a significant concept in resilience research. In response to new experiences and changes in the environment, the brain can change how it works and how it connects to other parts of itself. The brain is not a rigid and unchanging organ; it is adaptable and capable of transformation. This means that the brain can change and make new neural pathways that help it stay strong, even when things are hard.

The brain can heal and adapt so well after traumatic events. Neuroplasticity is the process by which new neural connections are formed and strengthened. When things get tough, the brain can turn on different parts that help with stress management, controlling emotions, and processing information. After that, these areas can form new connections and pathways, which helps us manage our emotions, think more clearly, and handle stress better.

Resilience science studies how stress hormones, especially cortisol, work. Long-term stress causes the body to release cortisol for a long time, which can damage the brain and make it less able to handle and respond to problems. We can control how our bodies respond to stress, which lowers cortisol levels and protects the brain from damage.

Being around kind and helpful people can also make your body release oxytocin, a hormone that helps you connect with and bond with other people. Oxytocin has been shown to make people feel safe, trusted, and like they belong, which can help their brains change and make them more resilient.

Learning about the science of resilience can help us figure out how to make ourselves more adaptable and better able to handle tough times. It shows that the brain is always growing and changing. Learning new skills, being mindful, getting social support, and keeping a positive attitude are all things that can help our brains become more flexible. This can make us more resilient and set us up for better health and success in life.

There are problems and setbacks in life that we can't avoid, and they can make us feel lost, discouraged, and unsure of what to do next. But we can get through these problems and come out stronger than before if we learn to be strong. Being resilient doesn't mean not having problems; it means being strong and flexible enough to handle and get through tough times.

To get over setbacks, it's important to have a growth mindset. Instead of seeing setbacks as failures or problems that will never go away, we can see them as chances to learn and grow. We need to remember that it's normal to have problems when we're learning, and they can teach us important things. When we see setbacks as steps on the way to success, we can face problems with curiosity and strength.

We should be good at solving problems. We need to actively look for solutions and take steps to fix the problem instead of getting stuck in a cycle of negative thoughts or worrying about it. This could mean breaking the problem up into smaller, easier-to-handle pieces, coming up with new ways to solve it, or asking people who have been through the same thing for help.

It is also very important to build emotional strength to get through hard times. We need to be emotionally strong enough to notice and accept how we feel without letting those feelings control us. We need to learn how to be kind to ourselves and accept ourselves, even when things are hard, because it's normal to feel a lot of different things. Building emotional resilience can help us bounce back from setbacks and stay healthy.

It's also important to keep things in perspective when things go wrong. You might forget about the bigger picture if you focus too much on your current problems. We need to be able to look at the situation from a different point of view. We should think about the things we've done well in the past and what has worked for us. This will help us stay positive and believe that we can make it through hard times.

To be resilient, you have to be willing to change and be open to new ideas. We often have to change our plans, goals, or expectations when things don't go as planned. We need to be willing to change and be ready to adjust our plans or how we do things when we need to. Life is always changing, and we can't always predict what will happen. Being able to adapt to new situations is a big part of being strong.

You need to see failures as a chance to learn and grow if you want to be more resilient. Failure is an unavoidable part of life, and being able to accept it and learn from it is important for building resilience and achieving success. We shouldn't be ashamed of or discouraged by failure. We should look at it as a chance to grow, learn, and get better instead. We can turn failure into a chance to succeed in the future by changing how we think about it.

Seeing failure as a chance to learn is one of the most important things you can do to accept it. We need to realize that failing gives us useful information and feedback that can help us improve and do well in the future. If we are interested in failure and want to learn from it, we can learn important lessons and change our plans. When we fail, we can reflect on ourselves and what we need to do to get better, learn new things, and try new approaches.

You also need to avoid being a perfectionist and start seeing yourself as someone who can learn and grow in order to accept failure. Because we want to be perfect, we often don't take risks or try new things because we're afraid of failing. We need to understand that we can never be perfect and that making mistakes is a normal part of learning. We believe in a growth mindset, which means that you can get better at things by working hard, making mistakes, and learning from them. When we accept that we are not perfect and work on having a growth mindset, we can stop being afraid of failing. This gives us more chances to grow and do well.

We need to remember that success isn't a straight line; it's a journey with bumps along the way. We need to realize that failing is often a necessary part of the process and that setbacks can be great chances to learn and change direction. When we accept failure, we can see success in a more complete and realistic way, one that includes the setbacks, challenges, and determination needed to get through them.

You need to be able to handle criticism from others or pressure from society. We should question the narrow definitions of success and find our own ways to measure growth and progress.

There is a lot of change and uncertainty in life, and being able to accept them is important for building resilience and getting through the world as it changes. People who are resilient don't fight or fear change and uncertainty. Instead, they see them as chances to learn, grow, and get better. We can adapt better, find new opportunities, and do well in changing situations if we accept change and uncertainty.

Resilience is very important for keeping relationships strong and healthy because every relationship has its ups and downs. To get through these problems and come out stronger, we need to have the right skills and attitudes. This will help us connect with others more deeply. You need to be able to talk to each other, show empathy, work out problems, and be open to learning and growing together in order to make relationships stronger.

Being able to talk to each other well is an important part of being strong in relationships. We need to make open and honest communication a top priority so that everyone feels safe talking about their worries, thoughts, and feelings (Bodenmann, G., 2017). We should try to understand other people's points of view and not judge them when they talk. We can solve problems and disagreements directly by encouraging people to talk to each other in a clear and polite way. This keeps problems from getting worse and helps everyone learn and grow together.

We need to put in a lot of effort to understand and accept how our spouses, partners, friends, and family members feel and what they've been through. We need to practice active empathy to build connections and support. This means putting ourselves in the other person's shoes. When we show empathy, we build trust, make our relationships stronger, and make it easier for us to get through tough times together.

You need to know how to settle disagreements to make your relationships stronger. We should not see conflicts as threats to the relationship; instead, we should see them as chances to grow and work through problems. We need to talk to each other in a way that helps everyone and find solutions that work for everyone and address everyone's needs and worries. We need to be willing to find common ground and be open to compromise while still being polite and understanding. When we handle conflicts well, we make our relationships stronger and better able to deal with problems that might come up in the future.

Being resilient in relationships also means being open to learning and growing as a person. It's important to remember that relationships need work and attention all the time. We need to look for opportunities to think about ourselves and figure out what we're good at and what we're not so good at. We should be open to hearing what others have to say and learning from our mistakes. We build a culture of resilience in our relationships by being open to learning and growing and having a growth mindset.

You also need to be able to handle your feelings well if you want to be strong in relationships. We need to learn how to manage our feelings by being aware of them and handling them in a healthy and helpful way. When we're angry or stressed, we shouldn't act on impulse or do things that are bad for us. We can deal with problems and keep our relationships healthy better when we keep our feelings in check.

Also, being strong in relationships means helping each other feel like they have a common goal and are there for each other. We need to know how important it is to be there for each other when things get tough. We should help our spouses, partners, friends, and family members feel better, encourage them, and give them peace of mind. We strengthen our relationships by helping each other and working together toward a common goal. This helps us get through hard times and come back stronger.

We build strong and healthy relationships by learning how to talk to each other, show empathy, work out problems, commit to personal growth, control our feelings, and create a sense of shared purpose and support. When both people are strong in a relationship, they can help each other grow, understand, and get through tough times. This makes for relationships that last a long time and are happy.

We need to build a resilience toolkit with a lot of different strategies and techniques so that we can handle the challenges and unknowns that life throws at us. These tools help us deal with stress, get back on our feet after things go wrong, and stay healthy in general. Even though everyone's resilience toolkit will be different, there are some basic strategies that can help you build a strong one.

Being resilient is being able to handle stress well. Long-term stress can harm our health and make it harder for us to get back on our feet after a setback. It's important to know how to handle stress in a good way. This could mean finding and doing things that help us relax, like deep breathing, writing in a journal, doing hobbies, or asking trusted friends for help. We can better deal with stress and stay strong when things get hard if we learn to recognize what stresses us out and how to deal with it in healthy ways.

You have to be able to solve problems to be strong. We can deal with setbacks better when we learn how to look at problems, find possible solutions, and do something about them. This means breaking problems down into smaller, easier-to-handle parts, coming up with other ways to solve them, and asking for help or advice when you need it. Having a solution-oriented mindset helps us deal with problems with confidence and adaptability, which makes us stronger when things get tough.

Another important part of a resilience toolkit is making and keeping a strong support network. When things get tough, it's good to have people you can trust to help you out, give you advice, and see things from a different angle. This network can include family, friends, mentors, or groups of people who help each other. We feel like we belong and are stronger when things get tough when we build strong relationships and encourage open communication with the people around us. We can get back on our feet much faster if we share our stories, ask for help, or just have someone listen to us.

You can become more resilient by being hopeful and thinking positively. We can get through hard times more easily if we keep a positive attitude and see problems as chances to learn and grow. This doesn't mean ignoring the truth about hard times; it means looking for solutions that will help and keeping a sense of hope and possibility.

In conclusion, the strength of resilience is an important part of being human which God deposited in us to deal with the problems and challenges that life throws at us.

Resilience is not a fixed trait; it is a trait that can change and grow over time. Neuroplasticity is the brain's ability to change and adapt in response to what it learns. This is the main idea behind resilience science. This knowledge helps us see failures as chances to learn and grow.

Building resilience is a lifelong process that requires effort, self-reflection, and a readiness to change. By putting the ideas and strategies from this chapter into practice, we can use the transformative power of resilience to reach our full potential to face challenges, thrive in the face of adversity, and live a more fulfilling and meaningful life.

CHALLENGE *Impulsive* THOUGHTS

We need to begin a journey of self-reflection and introspection to learn more about our impulsive thoughts and what causes them. To "Rewire Your Brain," you need to learn about the fascinating world of impulsive thoughts and how they can change our lives in big ways.

When we suddenly think of something, we might do it without thinking about it first. They can show up in a lot of ways, like making choices on the spot, getting mad for no reason, or acting without thinking. These automatic responses can have a big impact on our lives, including our mental health, relationships, and general quality of life.

To deal with impulsive thoughts in a helpful way, we need to notice them and give them a name when they happen. When we know what makes us react without thinking, we can pay more attention to our thoughts and feelings when things are happening. Understanding how our past experiences can change our thoughts can also help us figure out where these patterns came from and how they affect our thoughts now.

Our feelings often make us think about things. They can be very strong triggers that make our automatic reactions stronger and make it harder for us to make good choices. Looking into the complicated link between emotions and impulsive thinking can help us deal with strong feelings better.

Challenging impulsive thoughts is a strong way to change how we respond without thinking. We can put our thoughts to the test and see if they are true by thinking about other points of view. Cognitive restructuring can help us think more clearly and evenly, which will help us deal with the problems in our lives in a more planned and thoughtful way.

We should think about how important it is to question what we believe and see if what we believe is true. We can be more open-minded and strong in our thinking if we try to see things from other people's points of view.

We should always try to think critically about how to fix things. By getting better at not acting on our first thoughts, we can learn how to handle the good and bad times in life with clarity, wisdom, and emotional health.

We learn how to deal with impulsive thoughts in a new way as we go through this journey of change together. We need to "Rewire Your Brain" through the landscapes of our minds if we want to feel better emotionally.

Impulsive thoughts come to mind right away, and you don't think about them. You might do, feel, or decide things quickly without thinking about them first if you have these thoughts. They happen without us trying and can change the way we talk to people, make decisions, and act.

One reason why impulsive thoughts are important is that they happen right away. We don't have a lot of time to think about what they mean or if they're real because they happen so often. People can act on these thoughts without thinking, like buying something on a whim, taking a risk, or saying something without thinking about how it might affect other people. They can also be quick decisions, when we choose people or situations based on little information or our own biases.

Coming up with ideas quickly can change our lives in a big way. They can make people do things they don't want to do, hurt their relationships, and miss out on chances. If we act on our impulsive thoughts without thinking about what might happen, we could get bad results or feel bad emotions like guilt, shame, or disappointment.

Quickly coming up with ideas can also change the choices we make. They don't always use logical thinking or rational analysis, which makes us make decisions too quickly or without enough information. When you need to think things through carefully, like when you're trying to decide what to do with your money, your job, or a fight with someone else, this can be really bad.

How well we get along with other people can also be affected by our quick thoughts. When we make quick decisions or act on our automatic thoughts, we might not understand what other people mean, ignore their points of view, or get into fights for no reason. People may not understand each other, which can hurt their relationships and make them miss chances to show kindness and understanding.

You need to know what your impulsive thoughts are and how they affect you in order to get them under control. We can begin to figure out how to deal with these thoughts and change how we think about them by realizing that they come up on their own and not because we want them to. By looking into how impulsive thoughts affect us, we can learn more about how they can hurt us and try to find ways to make them less bad.

To challenge and modify our impulsive thoughts, we must first identify their nature and underlying causes. Automatic reactions are the things you think and do that seem to happen on their own. We don't think about them very often, but they can change our lives a lot.

You need to be more aware of yourself in order to notice when you're having impulsive thoughts. Being very aware of how we feel in different situations and what we say to ourselves is what it means.

For example, think about how a coworker, friend, or family member might give you good advice. You might automatically think, "They think I'm incompetent and don't value my work," if you're feeling insecure or afraid of failing.

It's helpful to stop and think about how we react to things right away if we want to find impulsive thoughts. You could do this by keeping a journal or writing down your thoughts when you feel strongly about something. We can start to understand how our automatic reactions work by paying attention to our thoughts and feelings without judging them.

It's also important to pay attention to the physical signs that come with having impulsive thoughts. Your heart rate may increase, your muscles may tense, or you may experience a sudden surge of adrenaline. If you know how these physical feelings work, you can tell when you're having impulsive thoughts.

There are a lot of things that can make someone think about things without really thinking them through. They could be linked to past events, worries, feelings of insecurity, or certain places. Someone who has been through a traumatic event before may have sudden thoughts when they are in situations that remind them of that event. Words or phrases that really get to you can also set you off.

We can learn about the reasons and patterns behind our automatic reactions by figuring out what makes us act on impulse. This information helps us find a way to change and question these thoughts that works.

There are often deeper reasons for our impulsive reactions that affect how we think and act. We can learn more about why we act on impulse and how to deal with these reactions better by looking into these roots.

We often do things without thinking because of what we've learned and how we've been raised. The things we do and the places we grew up shape how we think and act. If we grew up in a strict and authoritarian home, we might have learned to follow the rules and do what people in charge say right away. We might have thought it was okay to act on impulse or that it worked because we had seen it praised or rewarded before.

People often expect us to act a certain way, and when we see someone not doing what they should, it can make us do something without thinking. If we think that people are judging or criticizing us for not following the rules of society, we might do something without thinking. This is to keep us safe or get their approval.

When we act on impulse, our core beliefs and values can also change how we act. These strong beliefs change how we think about ourselves and the world around us. When we really believe that getting what we want right away or staying safe is more important than anything else, we are more likely to act on impulse. We might believe these things because of things that have happened to us, our culture, or our biology.

Some psychological factors can also make people act on impulse. Impulsivity is a principal symptom of conditions such as attention deficit hyperactivity disorder (ADHD) and borderline personality disorder (BPD). These conditions may arise from a combination of genetic, neurological, and environmental influences, making us more vulnerable to impulsive thoughts and actions.

When trying to figure out why we act on impulse, it's important to think about how our emotions affect us. Our feelings have a big impact on how we think and act. When we're scared, angry, or excited, we might do things without thinking. If we know what makes us feel a certain way and learn how to control our feelings, we can stop ourselves from acting on impulse.

To know why people act on impulse, you need to look at how different things work together. There are a lot of things that can make us act or think on impulse, such as how we were raised, what we learned, our social and cultural influences, our core beliefs, our mental health, and how we feel.

We can find better ways to deal with and change our automatic reactions when we learn more about what causes them. We can gradually mitigate the impacts of impulsive cognition and make decisions that are more rational and considered through practices such as self-reflection, therapy, and personal development.

Even when we act on impulse, our past experiences have a big impact on how we think, act, and respond. When we have sudden thoughts, we should think about what happened in the past that made us feel that way.

Things that have happened in the past can change the way you think and make you act on impulse. People who have been through a lot of bad or traumatic things may start to have negative thoughts about life.

You might say things like "the worst will happen" or "I know what happened" without thinking of other options when you think this way.

People who grew up in a place where their opinions were always ignored or invalidated may have thoughts of self-doubt that come to them quickly or always need other people to agree with them. These ways of thinking can change how people make choices and make them act on impulse to get quick approval or validation.

People can also think quickly when they've failed or had a setback before. Someone who has been let down or turned down a lot may be afraid of failing or feel like they need to do something quickly without thinking about what might happen. You might want to take risks or make decisions quickly without thinking them through when you're scared.

We can better understand how we react without thinking by learning how past events affect how we think about things. We can begin to question and modify our thoughts more constructively by identifying the experiences that have influenced them.

We can learn more about why we have impulsive thoughts by thinking about things that have happened to us in the past. We can grow as people and think more clearly and logically with this information. It helps us let go of the past and make better choices based on what's going on now instead of just reacting to what happened in the past.

Cognitive restructuring is a great tool that helps us change how we think and react automatically by using logical analysis. It means examining the fundamental concepts and convictions that result in impulsive thought processes and substituting them with more rational and equitable alternatives. We have more control over our thoughts and can make better choices when we do cognitive restructuring.

Cognitive restructuring is about figuring out how you act and think in different situations without really thinking about it. For this to work, you need to know and pay attention to how you think. By paying close attention to our thoughts, we can start to figure out what beliefs and assumptions are behind our impulsive reactions.

The next step is to carefully check to see if these automatic thoughts and beliefs are true after you know what they are. This means looking at the evidence that supports these ideas and thinking about other possible explanations and points of view. It is important to carefully check whether these ideas are true and fair, and to see if they are based on facts or distorted views.

One effective technique for cognitive restructuring is "evidence gathering," which involves systematically collecting evidence that either corroborates or refutes automatic thoughts and beliefs. By looking at how strong and reliable this evidence is, we can get a better idea of how true our first answers were. This process helps you get rid of cognitive biases and see things in a more fair and objective way.

We can also use logic to change how we react without even realizing it. This means checking our thoughts for any logical errors or cognitive distortions, such as making broad generalizations, jumping to conclusions, or assuming the worst. We can get rid of these wrong ways of thinking by questioning them and replacing them with more realistic and logical ones.

You should get rid of your automatic thoughts and replace them with new ones that are more balanced. One way to do this is to think of different ways to explain or understand what is happening. We can learn more and be more open-minded if we look at things from a few different angles. This process makes us think about how likely it is that good things will happen, what we can do about it, or other ways to look at the problem.

Challenging impulsive thoughts also means practicing and strengthening the new rational thoughts. You need to do it over and over again and be consistent to make the new ways of thinking stronger. Over time, we can learn to question our automatic responses and replace them with thoughts that make more sense and are more balanced.

Learning how to think logically is an important step in fighting impulsive thoughts and changing how you react automatically. People often have impulsive thoughts because their brains are wired in a way that makes them biased. They can make them believe and do things that don't make sense. If we work on having a more rational and balanced mind, we can make better decisions and control our impulsive thoughts better.

Learning how to find and question cognitive distortions is one of the best ways to make your thinking more rational. Cognitive distortions are things we do every day that change how we see things. Some cognitive distortions include black-and-white thinking (seeing things as either all good or all bad), overgeneralization (drawing broad conclusions from little evidence), and personalization (taking too much blame for things that aren't our fault). Once we know about these distortions, we can start to doubt their truth and replace them with more accurate and fair thoughts.

To think clearly, you need to know how to tell the difference between facts, guesses, and opinions. Based on what we know and what we think, our brains often come up with automatic thoughts. These thoughts might not be true and might be very personal. By carefully looking at the evidence and considering other explanations, we can get a better idea of what's going on. We should ask ourselves questions like, "What proof do I have to support this idea?" and "Are there other ways to explain what's happening?"

You need to be more open-minded and adaptable if you want to think more logically. It means being aware that our first thoughts and judgments aren't always correct or complete. We can better understand a situation and stop ourselves from acting on our first thoughts by looking for and thinking about other points of view. One way to do this is to use techniques like "perspective-taking," which means trying to see things from the other person's point of view.

You should also work on your ability to think critically if you want to be able to think more logically. This means being able to look at information without bias, find logical errors, and decide how trustworthy and accurate sources are.

We can question our quick thoughts and look at them in a more logical and reasonable way when we use critical thinking. A big part of this process is asking questions like "What proof backs up this thought?" and "Is this thought based on facts or guesses?"

You have to work hard and put in the time to learn how to think more clearly and fairly. You can improve by putting in the effort and thinking about yourself. By questioning our impulsive thoughts and changing how we react automatically, we can have more control over how we make decisions and live lives that are more fulfilling and meaningful.

In our daily lives, we often believe things and make guesses about them without really checking to see if they are true. These automatic thoughts can make you act on impulse because they might not have all the facts, be biased, or be based on memories that aren't true anymore.

If you have thoughts or feelings that make you act on impulse, you should stop and think about what you really believe. People often have strong beliefs that affect how they think and act without them even knowing it. We can find out if our assumptions are true and any cognitive distortions that might be there by questioning them.

To begin to question our assumptions, it can be helpful to find out what thoughts or beliefs are making us act without thinking. These thoughts could be things you say to yourself, things you think about, or pictures in your head that go along with the behaviour. We can look at these automatic thoughts more closely once we find them.

A good way to find out if our automatic thoughts are true is to look for proof that they are true and proof that they are not. This means looking at the facts and coming up with other ways to explain or understand what's going on. We can get a better view and stop our impulsive thoughts from taking over by going through this process.

It's also important to pay attention to how our automatic thoughts change how we feel. It's hard to think clearly and make decisions when we're feeling something. We can tell if our impulsive thoughts are good responses to the situation we're in right now by recognizing and understanding the feelings that cause them.

You can also talk to other people to see if your ideas are wrong. Talking about our automatic thoughts and beliefs with people we trust can help us think about things in a different way and come up with new ideas. People can change how we think by giving us new information or ways of looking at things that we hadn't thought of before.

We can also think about who we are and what we've done. If we take the time to think about our own cognitive biases, preconceived notions, and past experiences, we might be able to find any patterns or tendencies that make us think quickly. If we pay more attention to ourselves, we can get rid of these biases and think more clearly.

We can learn more about ourselves and the world by questioning what we think we know. When we act on impulse and do something about it, we can learn more about the cognitive biases and distortions that affect how we think. We can learn to think more clearly and fairly by going on this journey of self-reflection. This will make us feel better and help us make better decisions.

It's very important to look at things from different angles when you want to change how you react automatically and question your impulsive thoughts. When you have a narrow or biased view of the situation, you might think of things on the spur of the moment. We can learn more about what's going on by looking at things from different angles.

Thinking about how other people see things is one way to get different points of view. This means getting other people's opinions and feelings about the situation, even if they don't agree with you. By listening to what they have to say, we can learn more about ourselves and question any biases or assumptions that might be affecting our impulsive thoughts.

It's important to remember that looking for other points of view doesn't mean giving up what we believe or what we value. But it's a way to learn more and think about other things you could do. This process can help us be more open-minded and flexible in how we think about things. It makes us think about how set our quick thoughts are.

To really look for different points of view, you have to be interested and want to learn. This means being open to new ideas and figuring out how to talk to people who don't agree with you. Reading books from other cultures or talking to people who see things differently may also help you feel more empathy and understanding.

So, if you want to change how you think and how you react quickly, it's a good idea to look for different points of view. We can get a more balanced and nuanced view of the world by looking at things from different angles, thinking about other ways to interpret things, and actively looking for different points of view. This process helps people grow, learn to think critically, and become more understanding. This leads to better, more logical choices.

Impulsive thoughts often arise from hasty judgments and instinctive reactions lacking comprehensive reflection. If you want to stop acting on impulse, you need to learn how to solve problems that make you think. In this way, we can deal with hard times and make better decisions.

Knowing that your first thought might not be the best one is the first step to solving a problem. It could mean not doing what you first thought and instead using your brain to figure things out. First, you need to figure out what the problem is. If we can clearly define the problem, we can focus on finding the right answer instead of acting on impulse.

Once you know what the problem is, you need to get all the facts you need. This means looking at the situation from different angles, getting information, and thinking about it. Learning about the situation takes time, but it helps us understand it better, which can help us come up with better and more informed answers. It also helps to question any ideas or biases that could change your mind at the last minute.

If you know a lot about the problem and how it works, you can use critical thinking to come up with possible answers. This means using your imagination and coming up with a lot of different ideas. We can see a lot of different points of view and outcomes when we come up with a lot of different ideas. You should wait before making a decision right now and be open to all possible answers, even if they seem strange or go against what you first thought.

Now that you have a list of possible solutions, it's time to see if they can work and what might happen if they do. Thinking critically is a big part of this evaluation process. You should think about how helpful, useful, and maybe even harmful each solution could be for you and other people.

You need to stay calm and think clearly while you do this. Don't let your mind or heart get in the way. Don't let short-term gains affect your choice. You should instead look at the pros and cons of each choice objectively and think about how it will affect the future.

You can pick the best one after looking at all of them closely. You should make this choice based on your values, goals, and the results you want. You might have to give up something or come up with a solution that works for everyone. When we use critical thinking, we make better choices. This means we don't just do things because we want to or think they are right.

Putting the solution into action is the last step in solving a problem. You should make a list of what you need to do and what problems or challenges might come up. A good plan helps us stay on track and focused, which means we are less likely to get sidetracked by random thoughts or things that come up.

It's important to be aware of what's going on around you and inside you when you're trying to solve a problem. If you think about what you say and do on a regular basis, you might be able to change any patterns of impulsive behaviour. We can slowly get rid of our impulsive thoughts and make choices that are more rational and balanced by using our problem-solving and critical thinking skills on a regular basis.

We need to know that acting on impulse can have a big effect on our health and the choices we make. By recognizing their presence and effect, we have taken the first step toward getting back in control and living a life with more meaning and purpose.

Learning to notice automatic responses has been a big part of our journey. We know what makes us think on the spot, and this helps us keep them from taking over our lives. We can plan and think about how to respond better. Challenging impulsive thought has been shown to be a good way to change the way automatic responses work. By consciously questioning and changing our automatic reactions, we have given ourselves the power to adopt more balanced and constructive points of view.

As we finish this chapter, let's be happy about how far we've come in questioning our quick thoughts. We have taken back control of our lives, encouraged personal growth, and made our lives more meaningful and purposeful by changing how we automatically react.

We are now stronger, smarter, and more hopeful about how to deal with life's problems. We should accept this new information and keep going on our path to a life full of choices that are mindful, decisions that are empowered, and peace of mind.

DEVELOP and CULTIVATE *New* MEMORIES

Memories are an interesting part of how we think because they help us remember, retrieve, and make sense of a lot of things. "Rewiring Your Brain" can help you remember things better, whether you're a student who wants to do well on tests, a worker who needs to remember important information, or just someone who wants to remember things better in everyday life.

There are a lot of different ways we can help ourselves make and improve new memories. We can learn a lot about how to improve our memory, from how memories are made and stored to how to use memory aids and visualization to our advantage.

We need to learn the basics of how memories are made and how to get them back. We can make these processes better by learning more about how memories are formed and stored. It builds on this foundation by looking at ways to help us remember things better and recall them more easily. These methods can be used in a lot of different situations, which makes it easier for us to remember things and find them.

We should think about making mnemonic devices to help us remember things. These smart tools use pictures and connections to help us remember complicated ideas and facts. You can also use mind mapping and visualization to help you remember and organize information.

It's fun to learn new skills, and it gives us good ways to do it and remember them. Learning about the principles of skill acquisition and using certain techniques can help us remember things better and get more out of what we learn.

To keep our brains healthy, we need to keep them busy and active. There are a lot of memory games and brain exercises that can help us remember things and make our minds work better.

We need to learn how to keep learning for the rest of our lives. By encouraging people to keep learning, we make it possible for them to remember things better and grow as people. We can use helpful tips and tricks to keep this way of thinking for the rest of our lives.

The Bible says that we should make new memories by remembering how faithful God has been, letting go of our past problems, and being open to the new things He is doing. Memory isn't just about the past; it's a spiritual tool that can help you grow, heal, and have hope.

The Bible talks a lot about how strong memory is, not just for remembering the past but also for making the future. Making new memories is a way to refresh your spirit. "***Don't think about the past;***

forget about it," says Isaiah 43:18–19. "*Now it springs up; do you not see it*?" Look, I'm doing something new! This isn't a call to forget the past; it's a call to let go of things that don't help us so we can make room for new experiences of grace.

Memory is something that happens in the Bible. It's not just remembering; it's also telling stories, practicing the truth, and finding out who you are again. "*Think about the days of old and the generations that came before you*," says Deuteronomy 32:7.

Your father will tell you, and your older relatives will explain it to you. This verse shows that everyone has memories. We make new memories by listening to others, telling stories, and making traditions that show how great God is.

At the Last Supper, Jesus does this perfectly. In Luke 22:19, He breaks bread and says, "*Do this in memory of Me*." He tells His followers to remember the meal and the promise as well. We don't just remember when we take communion; we also make things new. Every time we tell it, it becomes more real.

Paul says something like this in Philippians 3:13–14: "*But one thing I do: I forget what is behind and push on toward what is ahead...*" Making new memories takes work. It means choosing to focus on what God is doing right now instead of what happened in the past. Philippians 4:8 says that it is a spiritual practice to teach the mind to think about what is true, good, and worthy of praise.

You can even change memories that hurt. Joseph names his son Manasseh in Genesis 41:51 and says, "*God has made me forget all my trouble and all my father's household*." This isn't denial; it's salvation. Joseph doesn't forget what happened to him; he just sees it differently. He lets new memories of healing, help, and leadership grow.

"I will remember what the Lord has done... I will think about all the great things You have done and all the things You have made." When you meditate, you remember things. When we think about what God has done and let it change how we live now, we make new spiritual memories.

Making new memories also means celebrating. Ecclesiastes 3 says, *"There is a time to laugh and a time to dance."* Sacred are happy times. They serve as spiritual reminders that God is always with us. When we spend time with people we care about, eat together, sing together, or celebrate important events, we make altars of thanks.

The Bible says that remembering is a duty and a gift. We should remember the right things, forget the right things, and make new memories that show how God is still working in our lives. Prayer, storytelling, worship, or reflection help us shape our minds so that we can keep what is good and let go of what we don't need anymore.

Memory formation and retrieval are important steps that let us encode, store, and get back information. By learning more about these processes, we can find ways to boost our memory and get the most out of our learning experiences.

The three main steps to making memories are encoding, consolidation, and retrieval. Encoding is how our brains change the information we get from our senses into a form that we can remember. This stage has attention, which helps us focus on important details, and elaboration, which helps us connect new information to what we already know (Kandel, Dudai, & Mayford, 2021).

Consolidation is what makes memories stronger and more stable. It mostly happens while you sleep and involves going over and over new information. At this point, memories are added to neural networks that are already there, which makes them harder to forget.

Retrieval is the process of getting to information that has been saved when you need it. The memory's cues, the person's mood, and the situation in which the information was learned can all have an effect on it. Retrieval cues are like triggers that make it easier for us to find the information we've saved.

There are a lot of ways to make memories and get them back. One effective method of learning is active learning, which involves engaging with and transforming the information rather than merely absorbing it. You can do this by writing down the main points, talking about them with other people, or teaching someone else what you know.

Another way is spaced repetition, which means going over information at longer and longer intervals. The spacing effect says that people remember things better when they go over them at different times instead of all at once.

You can also remember things better if you put them in order and organize them. You can connect related pieces of information in a way that makes it easier to find them later by making outlines, mind maps, or concept maps.

It's also important to know how feelings affect how memories are made. People tend to remember things better when they are emotionally charged, so finding ways to connect the information to your own feelings or experiences can help you remember it better.

You can improve your memory and recall in a lot of different ways, which will make it easier for you to remember and find information.

These techniques can help anyone who wants to remember things better, including students and professionals. These strategies can help people learn and remember better, which will make it easier and faster for them to understand information.

Spaced repetition is a great way to boost memory and recall. This method doesn't try to cram all the information into one session. Instead, it spreads out the learning and reviewing over time. When you study for short periods of time, like every few days, weeks, or months, your brain can strengthen the neural connections that are related to what you're learning. This repetition helps you remember things by putting them in long-term memory.

You can also use visualization and pictures as a way to do this. Our brains are very good at taking in visual information, and using this skill can help us remember things better. We can help ourselves remember things better by making clear mental pictures or connecting information to things we can see. For example, when you learn a new language, it can help you remember new words better if you picture things or places that go with them.

The chunking method can also help you remember and recall a lot. When you chunk information, you break it up into smaller, easier-to-handle pieces or "chunks." The brain can process and remember information better when it is grouped into groups that make sense. For instance, if you want to remember a long string of numbers, it can help to break them up into groups of three or four digits. This makes the job easier and helps you remember.

Using multisensory techniques in the classroom can also help you remember things and remember them. When you use more than one sense, like sight, sound, touch, smell, or taste, it can help your brain make stronger connections and remember things better. Reading out loud, highlighting important points while studying, or even using scented markers to mark up notes are all ways to add more sensory input that can help you remember things better.

Using mnemonic devices is a good way to boost your memory and help you remember things. Mnemonic devices help people remember things by connecting them to something that is easier to remember. These tools can be very helpful when you need to remember complex or abstract ideas, long lists, or sequences of information.

Using acronyms is a common way to remember things. You can do this by taking the first letter of each thing you want to remember and making a word or phrase out of it. To remember the order of the planets in our solar system (Mercury, Venus, Earth, Mars, Jupiter, Saturn, Uranus, and Neptune), you can say, "My Very Eager Mother Just Served Us Nachos." The first letter of each word in the sentence is the first letter of each planet.

Using memory aids can be a great way to remember things. Mnemonics are memory aids that help us remember things by connecting them to something else that is easier to remember. These tools can be acronyms, rhymes, or ways to picture things in your head.

The memory palace technique, or method of loci, is another way to help you remember things. This method connects things or ideas we want to remember with places we know well, like our home. We can remember things later by mentally going through each room and picturing the things we want to remember in those rooms. We can mentally go back through the space we know. This method uses our memory of where things are, which is usually better than our memory of abstract ideas.

The visualization method is also a great way to make strong and long-lasting mental images. If we picture things in a creative and exaggerated way, we can remember them better. To help us remember a list of groceries, we can picture a big banana dancing in the cereal aisle or a box of milk playing the piano. These pictures are more likely to stick in our heads because they are interesting and creative.

Mind mapping and visualization techniques can greatly enhance memory and aid in information retention (Buzan, T., 2020). These methods use pictures to show ideas, concepts, and relationships. This not only gets your creative juices flowing, but it also helps you learn better.

Mind mapping is a clear and structured way to put together and connect different pieces of information. This method helps us see the whole picture and how different ideas are related to each other. When we show our brains information in diagrams, colors, and symbols, they can remember and encode it better.

One of the best things about mind mapping is that it works with how our brains naturally work. The brain's natural ability to see patterns and make connections is what mind mapping is all about. We can connect and combine ideas in a more complete way with mind maps than with lists or linear notes.

You can use mind mapping and visualization along with other ways to remember things. For instance, we can use memory aids in our mind maps or connect pictures to certain bits of information. Not only do these methods make learning more fun, but they also make it easier and faster to remember and find information.

You need to be open and creative when you use mind mapping and visualization if you want to get the most out of them. We should give ourselves the freedom to look at different links and try out different ways to show things visually. It should be fun and meaningful for us to make mind maps and vivid mental pictures because this helps us remember things better in both ways.

You also need to practice mind mapping and visualization a lot to get better at them. The more we use these methods in our daily lives, the easier and more natural they will become. As time goes on, we'll learn how to think in pictures, which will help us make mind maps and mental images quickly. In many different situations, this will help you remember and understand information better.

Sleep is very important for memory consolidation, which is the process of making new memories stronger and less likely to fade away. When we sleep, our brains go through different stages, such as deep sleep and REM sleep. Each stage helps us remember things and make new memories in its own way. Understanding how sleep helps us remember things can help us learn and remember things more quickly and easily.

When you are in deep sleep, your brain goes through a process called slow-wave sleep (SWS). This stage is very important for declarative memory, which is the kind of memory that holds facts, events, and general knowledge. Research has shown that the brain actively reprocesses and strengthens newly formed memories during SWS, which helps them stay in long-term storage. SWS also helps to sort and rank memories, keeping the ones that are most important and getting rid of the ones that aren't.

REM sleep is connected to procedural memory, which is how we pick up new skills and habits. The eyes move quickly and the brain is more active at this stage. Studies have shown that REM sleep helps people remember new motor skills and complicated tasks better and lets them do them more smoothly when they wake up. During REM sleep, the brain does something called synaptic homeostasis. This helps strengthen and improve the neural connections that are important for learning how to move.

It's important to get enough sleep and develop good sleep habits in order to improve memory consolidation during sleep. Get the recommended seven to nine hours of sleep each night so your brain has enough time to go through the sleep stages it needs to process memories. It's also important to stick to a regular sleep schedule because it helps your memory work better.

Another way to use sleep to help your memory is to actively go over new information before you go to sleep. This method is called "sleep-dependent memory consolidation." It means going over and practicing what you've learned right before bed. This gives your brain a new set of memories to work on while you sleep, which makes it more likely that you will remember them well and keep them for a long time.

In addition to using sleep-dependent memory consolidation and optimizing sleep patterns, it is also important to make the sleep environment right. Make sure your bedroom is quiet, comfortable, and free of things that might keep you from sleeping well. Make a bedtime routine that helps you relax and tells your brain that it's time to go to sleep.

We can learn and remember new things much better if we understand and use the power of sleep to help us remember things. Getting enough sleep, using memory consolidation techniques that depend on sleep, and making sure your sleep environment is good can all help your memory encoding, retention, and overall cognitive function. Learning how to make and keep new memories includes learning how sleep affects memory formation.

You have to make the connections clear and easy to remember if you want to use a memory palace well. To help you remember a list of groceries, you could picture a big carrot in the doorway of your house, a carton of milk on the kitchen counter, and a loaf of bread on the couch in the living room. It's easy to remember what you need when you mentally walk through your memory palace and see how things are connected.

Memory palaces are just one type of spatial memory technique. They use pictures and spatial relationships to store and get information. For example, you can make mental maps or diagrams to help you remember things that are hard to remember. If you're learning about a historical event, you can make a map and mark important places, people, and events on it. This will help you understand the information.

They are great because they take advantage of our natural ability to remember things that are visual and spatial. They make us think and use our imaginations, which makes learning more fun and useful. We remember things better when we connect them to places or pictures we already know. This helps us make strong neural connections.

They can be helpful in a lot of different areas of learning. If you're studying for a test, learning a new language, or trying to remember a presentation, these tips can help you keep track of and remember things better. They help you organize your information and access it, which makes it easier to remember the details when you need them.

You are also more likely to interact with the material if you use memory palaces and other spatial memory techniques. Instead of just memorizing facts, you make mental pictures and connections, which makes the process of encoding stronger. Being involved helps us understand and remember things better, which makes our memories more complete and longer-lasting.

Crossword puzzles and word games are also good for your brain and can help you remember things. We need to remember words, make connections, and use language reasoning for these tasks. By making our brains remember certain words or finish word puzzles, we can improve our verbal memory, learn new words, and get better at connecting words and ideas.

Another good memory game that works on auditory and sequential memory is "Simon Says." "Simon says touch your nose" is an example of an order that a leader gives players. Players must remember and follow the order exactly. This game helps you improve your working memory and short-term memory by making your auditory memory stronger and your ability to remember and follow a sequence of information.

Brain games like Sudoku and logic puzzles can help you remember things and think more clearly. We need to use our logical reasoning and problem-solving skills to figure out the puzzles. Doing these exercises often will help us get better at remembering things, paying attention, and thinking critically.

There are also a lot of brain training programs and memory games that you can play on the internet and on your phone. These platforms have personalized exercises that work on specific cognitive skills, like memory. We can change the difficulty level of our training programs and keep track of our progress with these digital tools. This lets us make them fit our needs and preferences.

Not only do memory games and brain exercises help your brain right away, but they also make you feel good and accomplished. These things let us test our minds while having fun, lowering stress, and keeping a good attitude. Also, doing these games and exercises every day can help keep your brain healthy and stop it from getting worse over time.

A mindset of lifelong learning is a powerful way to keep our memory sharp throughout our lives (Lövdén, M., et al., 2021). It means having a positive and proactive attitude toward learning new things and skills, which can greatly improve our memory. When we have a lifelong learning attitude, we open ourselves up to many chances to grow as people, keep our minds active, and improve our memories.

One of the best things about having a lifelong learning mindset is that you are always learning new things and having new experiences. Our brains can make new connections and memories when we learn new things all the time. This is because learning gives our brains new ideas, concepts, and problems to solve. When we learn new things, like new hobbies, subjects, or jobs, our memories can change and grow.

A lifelong learning mindset also promotes an active and engaged approach to learning. We don't just passively take in information; we actively seek out new information and take part in the learning process. This active participation greatly enhances memory encoding by prompting us to contemplate and interrelate the information more profoundly. We make strong neural connections that help us remember and recall information by actively linking new information to what we already know and thinking critically.

Another good thing about having a lifelong learning mindset is that you can try out different ways and methods of learning. Learning new things or skills in different ways, like reading, listening to podcasts, going to workshops, or taking online courses, can help us remember things better. Each way of learning activates different parts of the brain. This makes memory pathways stronger and memory networks stronger and more connected.

Also, having a mindset of lifelong learning helps you see things in a way that helps you grow, which is important for memory improvement. We can believe that we can always make our memories better and bigger if we know that they aren't set in stone. When things get tough, this growth mindset tells us to keep going and use memory-boosting techniques that work. It helps us see memory improvement as a process that never ends, which makes us always look for new ways to make our memories work better.

Moreover, cultivating a lifelong learning orientation can produce various advantageous effects on overall brain health and cognitive functioning. Research suggests that engaging in intellectual activities and pursuing educational opportunities may reduce the risk of cognitive decline and age-related memory impairments (Verghese, J., et al., 2021).

Neuroplasticity is the brain's ability to change how it works and how it is built. Keeping our brains busy and challenged can help this process. This, in turn, helps you keep your memory sharp and even make it better over time.

There are many ways to help you remember and find information, such as making mnemonic devices and mind maps or using visualization techniques. Each has its own benefits. By using these tips when we learn and study, we can make the most of our brain power and remember things better.

We have also learned that sleep is very important for putting memories together. Getting enough sleep not only makes us feel better, but it also helps us remember things better by moving them from short-term to long-term memory storage. Getting enough sleep and rest can help us remember things better and learn new things.

We should always be learning and getting better at what we do. We have looked into ways to learn and remember new skills, and we have talked about how important it is to practice on purpose and work hard all the time. We can improve our memory over time and keep learning new things and getting better at what we already know by having a mindset of lifelong learning.

Memory palaces and other spatial memory methods have also been suggested as good ways to help people remember things. We can use our natural sense of space to build mental structures that help us remember things and find information. This spatial method can help us remember a lot of things and make our memory much better.

We have also looked into how brain games and memory exercises can help people think better. These things test our memory and give us chances to practice and get better. These fun exercises can help us remember things better and keep our brains healthy.

Finally, we talked about how important it is to always be learning. By being curious and looking for new information and experiences, we can keep our brains active and improve our memories. A dedication to learning and intellectual growth improves our lives and boosts our memory, allowing us to adapt and thrive in a world that is always changing.

DEVELOP POSITIVITY

Learning how to be positive is a very useful skill in a world that can seem full of problems, doubts, and bad news. It is a way of thinking that helps people handle the good and bad things that happen in life with grace, strength, and a sense of control. The benefits of promoting positivity go beyond just feeling good; they have a big impact on our mental and physical health, our relationships, and how we see the world in general.

Fostering positivity and its transformative effects can profoundly impact our lives. Optimism can change how we see the world in a number of ways. The science behind positivity, which looks at how it changes brain chemistry and how it can change the way we think, also helps us see "the light at the end of every dark tunnel."

Being thankful and showing gratitude are important ways to stay positive. By learning to enjoy and appreciate the good things in our lives, both big and small, we can make ourselves happy and content all day long.

Positive affirmations have also been shown to help us change how we see ourselves, boost our self-esteem, and make positive changes in our lives. These changes can help us keep peace and calm in our hearts and minds.

Negativity bias is the tendency to focus on the bad things in life. This can make it harder for us to be more positive. We can get over this bias and change how we think, which will help us see things in a more balanced and positive way.

Being around positive people and things is another important thing to think about. This is because the people and places we spend time with can have a big effect on our health and mood.

We need to find joy in our everyday lives. By being aware and looking for moments of beauty and inspiration, we can make our days happier and more meaningful.

Being kind to ourselves and having self-compassion helps us stay positive. To be mentally healthy and strong, we need to be kind and loving to ourselves.

You need to learn how to be strong and bounce back after a setback by thinking positively. We learn how to be strong and have a growth mindset by letting ourselves see problems as chances to learn and grow.

Having a positive attitude and spreading positivity to others can inspire and lift up the people around us. This makes the social environment friendly and helpful.

Being positive gives us a lot of options and is good for our health, relationships, and outlook on life. When we learn to be positive and tap into our own amazing potential, something big changes.

Having a good attitude is important for your health and can have a big impact on many areas of your life. A positive mindset is one that is hopeful, optimistic, and believes that one can face challenges and succeed.

How we see the world and how we feel, act, and think about life in general are all shaped by our beliefs and thoughts. A positive mindset means making a choice to look at the good things about people, situations, and experiences instead of the bad things.

We can change how we think and feel by noticing and questioning negative thoughts and replacing them with positive ones.

Your mental and emotional health is directly affected by how you feel about things. People who are positive tend to be less stressed, anxious, and sad. They can deal with problems, failures, and hard times better because they are strong, determined, and believe they can get through anything. This strength helps you deal with bad things better and makes you feel better mentally.

Studies have shown that keeping a positive attitude can have big benefits for your physical health (Miles A, et al. 2021). People who are optimistic usually have stronger immune systems, heal faster from injuries and illnesses, and are less likely to get long-term diseases like heart disease.

A positive attitude can make you feel good, which can help you take better care of yourself by getting enough sleep, eating well, and working out regularly.

When you have problems, having a good attitude helps you do something about them and find a way to fix them. People who have a positive attitude are more likely to see problems as chances to learn and grow when things get tough or go wrong. People who think this way are more creative, adaptable, and able to find good solutions, which makes them more productive and successful in many areas of life.

Positivity spreads. People who have a positive attitude tend to have and keep healthier relationships and social connections. People can feel better, the environment can be more peaceful, and people can connect on a deeper level if they have a positive attitude and good energy.

When we think about the good things in life, we can become more caring, understanding, and helpful. This makes our relationships with other people stronger and helps society as a whole.

A positive attitude gives you the drive and determination to keep going, which makes it easier to set and work toward goals. A good attitude helps you believe in yourself and stay focused on the chances of success when things go wrong or there are problems.

You are more likely to reach your personal and professional goals if you are determined and strong. This will make you feel more fulfilled and happy.

By actively using these strategies, we can develop a positive mindset and enjoy its many benefits in all areas of our lives. The power of optimism comes from the fact that it can change how people think, make them healthier, and make the future better and more satisfying.

To develop a constructive mindset, it is essential to engage in more than mere positive thinking; one must also comprehend the impact of positivity on brain chemistry and the underlying scientific principles. Neuroscience research has uncovered the fascinating connection between positive emotions and the brain, highlighting the numerous benefits of promoting positivity (Seligman, M. E. 2018).

When we feel good, like when we're happy, thankful, or in love, our brains change in ways that are good for our health. Dopamine, which is often called the "feel-good" chemical, is a big part of this process.

Dopamine is connected to feelings of happiness, motivation, and reward. Dopamine is released in our brains when we do things that make us happy and satisfied, like spending time with people we care about or doing things we enjoy.

Also, positive feelings have been shown to activate the prefrontal cortex, which is the part of the brain that controls executive functions like making decisions, planning, and solving problems. This activation makes our brains work better, helps us pay attention, and makes us smarter in general.

Positive feelings also help the brain make new connections and encourage neuroplasticity, which is the brain's ability to change and grow throughout life. This means that if we often feel good things, we can actually change our brains to be more open to good things and improve our mental health as a whole.

In addition to the immediate alterations in brain chemistry, cultivating a positive attitude over time yields numerous long-term advantages. Studies show that people who often feel good tend to be healthier, less stressed, and less likely to have mental health problems like anxiety and depression (Park SQ, et al. 2017).

Positive emotions are linked to better heart health, a stronger immune system, and a longer life.

The science of positivity also talks about emotional contagion, which is when our feelings can spread to other people and change how they feel. When we spread positivity, it can have a ripple effect, making the social environment more positive and supportive for everyone. This shows how important it is to be positive for both our own health and the health of those around us.

Learning about the science behind positivity can be a good reason to make positive changes in our daily lives. We can use the power of positivity to start a virtuous cycle of happiness and well-being by looking for positive experiences, doing things that make us happy, and being grateful and appreciative on purpose.

We can learn a lot about how being positive can make us healthier, smarter, better at socializing, and happier overall by learning about the link between good feelings and brain function. We can use this information to make smart choices and work on having a better attitude, which will make us happier and more satisfied in the long run.

Being thankful and grateful can make you feel better and help your health (Emmons, R. A., & Mishra, A., 2021). It means making a point of noticing and thanking the good things in life.

Being thankful means being aware of and grateful for the good things in our lives, no matter how big or small they are. It means being thankful for the people, things, and experiences we have now. Being thankful helps us remember what we already have instead of what we don't have, which makes us feel better.

Practicing gratitude on a regular basis can be good for our mental, emotional, and physical health in many ways. Research has shown that gratitude can help with stress, sleep, self-esteem, empathy, compassion, relationships, and maybe even the immune system (Wood, A. M., et al., 2019). It helps us look at life in a more positive and hopeful way.

We keep a gratitude journal by writing down three to five things we are thankful for every day. This habit makes us look for good things and be grateful for them. Saying thank you for a beautiful sunset, a friend who is there for you, or a good meal is all it takes.

Writing thank-you notes to the people who have made our lives better can mean a lot. It helps us show how much we care and makes our connections with other people stronger. Whether we send them or keep them, writing letters can have a big impact on our health.

Taking a few minutes every day to think about what we're thankful for can be very helpful. You can do it while you're praying, meditating, or just taking a moment to enjoy the now. By consciously focusing on the good things, we teach our minds to notice and appreciate the abundance in our lives.

It's not just about doing certain exercises to be grateful; it's also about changing how you think to be grateful. This means that you should make it a habit to look for the good in every situation, even the tough ones. It's about changing how we think about things and looking for the good in them. This can help us grow and make sense of tough times.

Not only does saying thank you help us, but it also helps others. Telling our friends, family, and coworkers how much we care about them can make our relationships stronger and make the world a better place. When we show thanks to others, we help start a cycle of positivity and encourage them to start their own gratitude practices.

Positive affirmations are strong words that help us change our minds from negative to positive. They help us change how we think and what we believe, which makes us more positive and strong in how we see the world. By consciously and consistently using positive affirmations, we can use our power to change things and get a lot of benefits.

Positive affirmations change the way our subconscious mind thinks, which is what shapes our beliefs, attitudes, and actions. When we say affirmations over and over again, we start to change the way we think about things that are bad and replace them with thoughts that are good and give us power. This rewiring process helps us think more positively over time.

Affirmations are a great way to boost your confidence and make you feel better about yourself. When we see the good things about ourselves, we feel better about ourselves and believe in our abilities. This increase in self-confidence can help us in many areas of our lives and make us happier.

Positive affirmations can help us stay strong when things get tough. When things get tough, we can be more positive by remembering how strong we are, how resilient we are, and how we can get through tough times. Affirmations can help us stay on track, stay motivated, and keep going, which makes it easier to deal with problems.

Affirmations are very important for having a good attitude. We train our minds to focus on the good things in life by saying good things over and over again. We can now look at problems with hope, see opportunities in them, and stay hopeful thanks to this change in how we think.

Affirmations that are positive can really help us stay motivated and focused on our goals. When we believe in ourselves, affirm our ability to succeed, and stay committed to our goals, we build our resolve and determination. This higher level of motivation pushes us forward and helps us get through problems and reach our goals.

Affirmations are good for our mental health. Saying nice things over and over can help us feel better. Affirmations can help you feel better by replacing stress, anxiety, and bad feelings with calm, confidence, and hope. This better mood is good for your health and happiness.

Positive affirmations can also help us get along better with other people. When we use affirmations that encourage kindness, compassion, and understanding and work on having a positive mindset, we feel better about ourselves. People can talk to each other better, feel closer to each other, and get along better when they have this positive attitude.

To get the most out of positive affirmations, we need to say them clearly and positively, as if the outcome we want is already happening. You could say something like, "I can do everything and I am sure of it."

At least a few times a day, say your affirmations over and over again. Repetition helps us remember the good things we say. Believe the affirmations you choose. Accept them with all your heart, and let yourself really believe the good things you say.

Picture and feel the good result as you say your affirmations. Using your senses makes the experience more real and interesting, which makes the good beliefs stronger. Make sure that your affirmations are in line with your own dreams, goals, and values. You can make affirmations more meaningful and helpful for your journey by making them your own.

You can change your mind, get healthier, and reach your full potential for a happier and more fulfilling life by making positive affirmations a part of your daily routine and believing in their power.

Things that happen to us every day can make us feel bad or think bad things. This negative bias, which is a normal part of the human mind, can make good things seem less important and keep people from growing. But we can actively promote positivity and improve our health if we understand and get past this bias.

Positivity and negativity are not just feelings; they are spiritual attitudes that shape our perceptions of God, ourselves, and the world. The Bible doesn't say these exact words, but it does say that our thoughts, words, and attitudes can have a big impact. The Bible says that a heart that is thankful, hopeful, and trusting can bring blessings, but a heart that is full of complaints, fear, or bitterness can stop spiritual growth.

In Numbers 13, Moses sends twelve spies to Canaan to check it out. Ten come back with bad news: "*We can't attack those people because they're stronger than us.*" People in the camp start to complain because of their fear.

But two men, Joshua and Caleb, look at the same land and say, "*We should go up and take it, because we can.*" The facts are the same; it's the way you see them that is different. The ten see giants and loss, but the two see chances and hope.

This story shows how bad thoughts can keep a group from moving forward, while good thoughts based on faith can help it move forward.

Paul says in Philippians 4:8, "*Think about things that are true, good, right, pure, beautiful, admirable, or great.*" This isn't just being hopeful. Thinking about things that show how good God is is a spiritual practice. Paul writes this from prison, which shows that being positive is not a matter of luck; it is a choice.

Elijah is very scared and sad in 1 Kings 19. He runs away into the woods and says, "*I've had enough, Lord.*" "*Give me my life.*" There is no doubt that he has a bad attitude. But God doesn't yell at him; instead, he gives him a break, food, and a soft voice.

Elijah's story shows us that it's not a sin to be negative; it's just human. But it needs to be given to God so that it can be changed. Elijah doesn't feel bad because of God; He heals him.

Jesus is a good example of this balance. He cries at the grave of Lazarus in John 11. He feels the weight of sadness. But then He tells Lazarus to come out and live again. His emotional honesty does not diminish his power; rather, it enhances it. Being positive for Jesus doesn't just mean being happy all the time. It means having a strong belief that resurrection is possible, even when death is close.

Negativity can change the truth if it isn't kept in check. His friends keep telling him that his pain is punishment in the story of Job. Their strict, negative theology stops them from seeing grace. Job, on the other hand, keeps fighting with God even though he is hurting.

In the end, God tells the friends off and praises Job for being honest. This shows us that being negative because of judgment is bad, but being sad because of a relationship can lead to revelation.

The Bible says in Proverbs 17:22, "*A cheerful heart is good medicine, but a crushed spirit dries up the bones.*" Being positive heals you in every way, not just mentally. It's not about pretending everything is okay; it's about choosing joy as a sign of faith.

In Matthew 12:34, Jesus says, "*For the mouth speaks what the heart is full of.*" What we say shows how we really feel. Being positive or negative isn't just a mood; it's a reflection of what we believe. Speaking life puts us in line with God's creative power. When we talk about death, we repeat what the enemy has twisted.

The Bible tells us to develop an attitude of gratitude. 1 Thessalonians 5:18 says, "*Give thanks in all situations; this is God's will for you in Christ Jesus.*" Gratitude is the ground where good things grow. It doesn't ignore hard times; instead, it looks at them through the lens of grace.

The Bible tells us to choose the posture of praise, whether we are facing giants in the land, grief in the tomb, or weariness in the wilderness. Being positive isn't stupid; it's prophetic. It looks beyond the present to the future. And when you give your negative thoughts to God, they can be the beginning of change.

Negative bias is when you pay more attention to bad information than good information. This bias is deeply rooted in our evolutionary past because our ancestors had to put potential threats first to stay alive.

This bias was helpful in the past, but it can be bad now that bad things and feelings often take up our time.

To get rid of negative bias and promote positivity, it's important to be aware of our thoughts and consciously change them. Cognitive restructuring is a good way to get rid of bad thoughts. It means finding those thoughts, questioning them, and replacing them with thoughts that are more positive and realistic. We can slowly change how we think by questioning the truth of negative beliefs and looking for proof that positive ones are true.

It's also important to be nice to yourself to get rid of negative bias. It means being nice to ourselves, understanding ourselves, and accepting ourselves, even when we make mistakes or say bad things about ourselves. Recognizing and validating our feelings can help us have a positive internal conversation that fights negative bias and helps us grow as people.

It's important to make the world around us a better place that helps us become better people. Friends, family, and communities that support and lift us up can have a big impact on how we think. These good relationships give us a network of people who can help us, encourage us, and inspire us. This can help us get over bad feelings and see the world in a better light.

If we work hard to get rid of negative bias and spread positivity, we can get a lot of good things. Being positive can help you feel better mentally and emotionally, make you more resilient, and make you happier with your life as a whole. Being positive not only helps us, but it also helps the people around us.

We can get past the limits of negativity bias by actively fighting negative thoughts, being aware of them, being nice to ourselves, and being around positive people. Being positive makes us happier, stronger, and more satisfied, and it also helps us spread positivity to others.

It's important to be around positive people if you want to stay positive. The people and places we spend time with have a big effect on our health, thoughts, and feelings. If we choose to spend time with positive people, we can improve our own positive outlook and have a better chance of living a happier and more fulfilling life.

Look at the people you spend time with as one of the first things you should do to be around positive people. Consider the people you spend the most time with and how they make you feel. Do they help you feel better and give you hope? Do they make you feel good and help you become a better person? It can be very empowering to be around people who have these traits.

Positive people are usually hopeful, help others when things get tough, and give constructive criticism when it's needed. Their good energy can make you want to think and feel the same way as they do.

It's not just the people we are with that shape our thoughts and feelings; it's also the places we spend time in. Think about the places you spend time, like your home, your job, or your social life. Do these places make you feel good, inspired, and at ease?

Making your home and work environment reflect your values and promote positivity can have a big impact on your health and happiness. You could add things that make you feel good, like plants, bright colors, meaningful art, or natural light.

Things that make you feel good can help you remember to stay positive every day.

In addition to the people you hang out with and the places you go, it's also important to choose positive influences through different media channels. Be careful about what you read, watch, or listen to, whether it's books, articles, social media, or TV shows.

Pick things to read, watch, and listen to that make you feel good and give you ideas. Learn about people who have had hard times and become better people, and see acts of kindness. Reading happy stories can help you learn to focus on the good things in life and get ideas from what other people have done.

You might also want to join groups and communities that have the same values and interests as you. Being around people who think like you and want to get better and think positively can help you a lot. These groups often give you chances to work together, learn, and grow. This can help you change how you think about things and make your positive attitude stronger.

It's important to keep in mind that not everything that happens in life will be good all the time. There will always be issues, mistakes, and bad things that happen. But you can build resilience and find ways to get through hard times with hope and strength by being around positive people and things on purpose. People who are good for you can help you remember what you can do and give you the strength to get through tough times.

Being around people who are positive themselves is a great way to stay positive. You can make your life more positive by evaluating and improving your relationships, making your surroundings more positive, choosing positive media to consume, and joining supportive communities.

If you actively look for these kinds of influences, you can get healthier, become stronger, and have more fun and personal growth. Remember that being happy spreads. When you spend time with positive people, you not only help yourself, but you also help everyone else.

In the busy world we live in today, it's easy to get caught up in our daily routines and forget about the little things that make us happy. But actively looking for and finding joy in everyday life can have a big effect on our health and happiness (Seligman, M. E., 2018).

You have to change how you think about things and be open to seeing the beauty and goodness in even the smallest things to find joy in everyday life. It's about being present and letting ourselves fully connect with the people and things around us. This can make us feel better and more content in general.

We stop worrying about what's wrong or hard and start thinking about what's going well when we regularly think about what we're thankful for. If we change the way we look at things, we can find happiness in all the good things around us, which will make us happier and more content.

To be happy in life, we need to do things that make us happy. These activities can be very different for everyone. They could be hobbies, creative projects, time spent outside, or time spent with family and friends. Putting our health first and making time for things that make us happy makes it easier for happy moments to happen.

We give ourselves the power to find and enjoy the happy moments that are always there, even when things are hard, by changing how we think about bad things and focusing on the good things about any situation. If we learn to be strong and have a good attitude, we can get through the ups and downs of life with grace and find happiness even when things are hard.

It's not about waiting for big happy things to happen; it's about noticing and enjoying the little things that make you happy every day. Practicing mindfulness, gratitude, doing things that make us happy, and having a positive attitude can help us enjoy the little things in life more and feel happier and more positive overall. Remember that joy isn't something that just happens to us; it's something we actively look for and make happen in our lives.

Being nice is a basic part of being human that can change our lives and the lives of others. You need to do things on purpose and on a regular basis that make you and others feel compassion, empathy, and understanding in order to grow kindness. When we choose to put kindness first in our lives, we set off a chain reaction of good things that affect more than just how we treat other people.

Being kind is good for our health in many ways. Many studies have shown that doing nice things makes the body release oxytocin, which is often called the "love hormone." Oxytocin makes people feel happy, lowers stress and anxiety, and strengthens social ties (Tan TT, et al. 2021). If we are kind to others on a regular basis, we can feel happier, have better mental health, and get along better with the people around us.

Being kind can be as simple as doing little things or as big as doing big things. A small act of kindness, like holding the door for someone, giving them a real compliment, or really listening to a friend in need, can make a big difference in their day. Paying for a stranger's coffee or volunteering at a local charity are two examples of random acts of kindness that can have a big impact on both the giver and the receiver.

Being nice also makes the world a better place because it makes it more friendly and helpful. People want to be nice to us when we are nice to them. Being kind to others can have a big effect on them, and even small acts of kindness can make them more likely to be kind to the people they meet. This starts a cycle of good feelings that spreads through communities and makes the world a better place.

Being kind helps you get to know people better and makes your relationships stronger. When we show kindness and empathy to others, we build trust and understanding. Kindness helps us look past our differences and brings us together, which is a good thing. Being nice to each other can make a relationship stronger, make it easier to talk to each other, and make the atmosphere more loving and peaceful.

Look at the people you spend time with as one of the first things you should do to be around positive people. Consider the people you spend the most time with and how they make you feel. Do they help you feel better and give you hope? Do they make you feel good and help you become a better person? It can be very empowering to be around people who have these traits. Positive people are usually hopeful, help others when things get tough, and give constructive criticism when it's needed. Their good energy can make you want to think and feel the same way as they do.

It's not just the people we are with that shape our thoughts and feelings; it's also the places we spend time in. Think about the places you spend time, like your home, your job, or your social life. Do these places make you feel good, inspired, and at ease?

Making your home and work environment reflect your values and promote positivity can have a big impact on your health and happiness. You could add things that make you feel good, like plants, bright colors, meaningful art, or natural light.

In the busy world we live in today, it's easy to get caught up in our daily routines and forget about the little things that make us happy. But actively looking for and finding joy in everyday life can have a big effect on our health and happiness (Seligman, M. E., 2018).

You have to change how you think about things and be open to seeing the beauty and goodness in even the smallest things to find joy in everyday life. It's about being present and letting ourselves fully connect with the people and things around us. This can make us feel better and more content in general.

CONCLUSION

We learned a lot from the book "Rewire Your Brain" about how our brains can change. We learned about how our brains can change and grow in amazing ways as we get older. Changing the way our brain pathways work can have a big impact on our happiness and health, we learned.

Neuroplasticity demonstrated that our brains are capable of change and growth, rather than remaining static. We learned how to do different exercises and how to change the way we think so that we don't always do the first thing that comes to mind. This helped us grow as people.

We told them that it's important to stand up for what we believe in and that the stories we tell ourselves can change our lives. If we work hard, we can learn how to keep our minds strong and our thoughts in check. This will help us get through tough times and find ways to make things better.

On this trip, we learned how to stay positive and not let our feelings get the best of us. We learned that our emotions, ideas, and intelligence can all affect the decisions we make. If we knew more about these parts of our minds, we could make choices that fit with our values and goals.

We learned that sleeping enough, exercising, eating well, and handling stress are all good for our brains and minds. Making healthy choices is the best way to change our brains and make changes that last.

We are ready to change our lives because we know about neuroplasticity and how to change our minds to make things better.

The rest of the book went into even more detail about how to make our brains work better, remember things better, and become smarter. We will keep looking into how strong our minds are and how we can use that strength to make long-lasting changes.

We can change how our brains work and get past the limits of negativity if we are dedicated, persistent, and committed to becoming better people. Things will get better for us after the change, and our lives will have more meaning. We will be in charge of our own happiness.

We also talked about how feelings are hard to understand and how they change the way we think and act. We began a long journey to learn how to deal with our feelings and become stronger. We learned how to deal with problems in life with strength and grace.

We learned a lot about how our brains work and how to use our emotions to get through tough times. When we got emotionally smart, we learned how to deal with our feelings in a kind and smart way. We couldn't just do it; we had to make plans for what we were going to do.

We learned how to deal with our feelings better by doing a lot of different activities and exercises. This made it possible for us to talk about them and handle them in a way that worked for us. We learned that we should take care of ourselves and be kind to ourselves. We learned that taking care of our mental health is important because it can help us change how our brains work and keep us positive.

Being strong was a big part of our journey. This means that even when things don't go as planned, change, or get hard, you can still do well. We learned that having a growth mindset can help us see problems as chances to learn and improve. We were able to keep going and fix things because we saw our mistakes as chances to learn and get better.

We also learned how important it is to have family and friends who can help you out when you need it. Our relationships with other people helped us, made us feel better, and gave us the strength to keep going when things got hard. We need to work on our minds and help each other in our communities if we want to have strong minds.

We also talked about how we're almost done with our journey to change ourselves and be open to good things. We talked about how memories can change how we feel, think, and believe in general. We learned how to make new memories and use them to change the way we think and see things.

We learned about memory and how to use it to help us remember things. This taught us that our brains can change the way we think about and remember things. We learned that memories can change over time. How we feel, think, and see things can change them. With this information, we could change the bad things we said to ourselves and get rid of beliefs that were holding us back from growing. Instead, we picked new stories that made us feel strong.

We learned how to make and keep good memories by doing a lot of different things and working with our hands. We changed how our brains work when we thought about times when we were happy, thankful, and successful. It made sense that we felt stronger and more hopeful. We found out that being positive changed everything about us, from how we think and feel to how we act. We felt better and more at ease.

We also learned more about how our memories, emotions, and thoughts all work together. We learned that the way we remember things changes how we see and believe things, and the way we think and feel changes how we remember things. We helped start a good cycle by getting people to think and feel good things. We can learn and become better people from this cycle of happy memories.

"Rewire Your Brain" changed our lives, and now that we've finished reading it, we're celebrating how far we've come in changing our minds and accepting the power of good memories. We now know how to get stronger, remember things better, and control our emotions. We can make changes that will last and make us happy because of all of these things.

But this isn't the end of our journey. It says that you should always try to be a better person and be happy. As we get older, our brains change and grow because they can. We have to work hard and be dedicated to changing our brains and making our good thoughts stronger.

Remember what we've learned and what this book has taught us as we think about things. We should keep our promise to think about our quick thoughts, back up our own ideas, control our minds, and feed our brains. We need to keep getting stronger, learn how to deal with our feelings, and make memories that change the way we see things.

REFERENCES

Adams, K., et al. (2021). Chronic Inflammation in the Etiology of Disease across the Life Span. In Mechanisms of Chronic Disease: Key Perspectives (pp. 43-67). Springer.

Ames, B., et al. (2021). A critical evaluation of the role of vitamin E in neurodegenerative diseases. BioFactors, 47(1), 49-65.

Begum, N., & Richardson, M. (2020). Vitamin B6 and cognitive development: Recent advances and future directions. Nutrients, 12(11), 3343.

Bodenmann, G. (2017). Dyadic coping and its significance for marital functioning. In P. Noller,

G. Karantzas, & G. A. Baxter (Eds.), The Wiley-Blackwell Handbook of Couples and Family Relationships (pp. 275-291). Wiley-Blackwell.

Büsing A, et al. (2021). Awe/gratitude as an experiential aspect of spirituality and its association to perceived positive changes during the COVID-19 pandemic. frontiersin.org/articles/10.3389/fpsyt.2021.642716/ful

Buzan, T. (2020). The Mind Map Book: Unlock Your Creativity, Boost Your Memory, Change Your Life. Pearson Education Limited.

Buzan, T. (2021). Mind Maps, Memory Palaces, and Other Techniques for Unlocking Your Memory and Boosting Creativity. Pearson.

Damasio, A. (2018). The Strange Order of Things: Life, Feeling, and the Making of Cultures. Pantheon Books.

Damasio, A. R. (2020). The Strange Order of Things: Life, Feeling, and the Making of Cultures. Vintage.

Davis, S., et al. (2018). Choline: Exploring the Growing Science on Its Benefits for Moms and Babies. Nutrition Today, 53(6), 268-277.

Duckworth, A. L., Peterson, C., Matthews, M. D., & Kelly, D. R. (2007). Grit: Perseverance and passion for long-term goals. Journal of Personality and Social Psychology, 92(6), 1087- 1101.

Emmons, R. A., & Mishra, A. (2021). Why Gratitude Enhances Well-being: What We Know, What We Need to Know. In Handbook of Well-Being (pp. 1-27). Noba Scholar.

Fishman MDC. (2020). The silver linings journal: gratitude during a pandemic. sciencedirect.com/science/article/pii/S1546084320300869?via%3 Dihub

Fox GR, et al. (2015). Neural correlates of gratitude. frontiersin.org/articles/10.3389/fpsyg.2015.01491/full

Gallagher S, et al. (2021). Gratitude, social support and cardiovascular reactivity to acute psychological stress.

sciencedirect.com/science/article/abs/pii/S0301051121000831?via%3Dihub

Gollan JK, et al. (2016). Twice the negativity bias and half the positivity offset: evaluative responses to emotional information in depression.sciencedirect.com/science/article/abs/pii/S000579161530 0252?via%3Dihub

Guerrera, M., et al. (2018). Therapeutic uses of magnesium. American Family Physician, 97(10), 649-650.

Harrison, F., et al. (2022). Vitamin C function in the brain: Vital roles in synaptic transmission, oxidative stress, and neurodevelopmental disease. Journal of Neuroscience Research, 100(3), 830-847.

Jans-Beken L. (2021). A perspective on mature gratitude as a way of coping with COVID-19. frontiersin.org/articles/10.3389/fpsyg.2021.632911/full

Jernerén, F., et al. (2020). Omega-3 fatty acid treatment in 174 patients with mild to moderate Alzheimer disease: OmegAD study: A randomized double-blind trial. Archives of Neurology, 69(7), 915-923.

Johnson, R., et al. (2019). The Mediterranean Diet: An Evidence-Based Approach. Springer.

Jones, B., et al. (2020). Dietary Antioxidants and Cognitive Function: A Review of Clinical Evidence. Nutrients, 12(1), 29.

Kahneman, D. (2011). Thinking, Fast and Slow. Farrar, Straus and Giroux.

Kandel, E. R., Dudai, Y., & Mayford, M. R. (2021). The Molecular and Systems Biology of Memory. Cell, 184(5), 1280-1296. doi:10.1016/j.cell.2021.01.035

Lövdén, M., et al. (2021). Cognitive aging and training: Insights from the ACTIVE Study. Current Directions in Psychological Science, 30(2), 208-215.

Masten, A. S. (2018). Resilience theory and research on children and families: Past, present, and   promise. Journal of Family Theory & Review, 10(1), 12-31.

Mathers N. (2016). Compassion and the science of kindness: Harvard Davis lecture 2015.bjgp.org/content/66/648/e525

Miles A, et al. (2021). Using prosocial behavior to safeguard mental health and foster emotional well-being during the COVID-19 pandemic: A registered report protocol for a randomized trial. journals.plos.org/plosone/article?id=10.1371/journal.pone.0245865

Mosewich, A. D., Crocker, P. R. E., Kowalski, K. C., & DeLongis, A. (2018). Applying self-   compassion in sport: An intervention with women athletes. Journal of Sport and Exercise Psychology, 40(3), 126-137.

Oliveira R, et al. (2021). The impact of writing about gratitude on the intention to engage in prosocial behaviors during the COVID-19 outbreak.frontiersin.org/articles/10.3389/fpsyg.2021.588691/full

Park SQ, et al. (2017). A neural link between generosity and happiness. nature.com/articles/ncomms15964

Rahman, A., et al. (2021). Zinc: A Critical Review of Its Role in Human Health and Nutrition. International Journal of Preventive Medicine, 12(1), 107.

Sansone RA, et al. (2010). Gratitude and well-being. ncbi.nlm.nih.gov/pmc/articles/PMC3010965/

Sciara S, et al. (2021). Gratitude on social media: a pilot experiment on the benefits of exposure to others' grateful interactions on

Facebook.frontiersin.org/articles/10.3389/fpsyg.2021.667052/full

Segal, Z. V., Williams, J. M. G., & Teasdale, J. D. (2018). Mindfulness-Based Cognitive Therapy for Depression (Second edition). Guilford Press.

Seligman, M. E. (2018). The Hope Circuit: A Psychologist's Journey from Helplessness to Optimism. Hachette UK.

Smith, J., & Johnson, A. (2022). The Role of Nutrition in Brain Health and Cognitive Function. Journal of Nutritional Neuroscience, 25(3), 145-158.

Tan TT, et al. (2021). Mindful gratitude journaling: psychological distress, quality of life and suffering in advanced cancer: a randomized controlled trial. spcare.bmj.com/content/early/2021/07/07/bmjspcare-2021-003068

Verghese, J., et al. (2021). Leisure activities and the risk of amnestic mild cognitive impairment in the elderly. Neurology, 76(16), 1435-1442.

Williams, M., et al. (2023). Gut-Brain Axis: The Microbiota-Gut-Brain Connection and Its Role in Neuropsychiatric Disorders. In The Gut-Brain Axis: Dietary, Probiotic, and Prebiotic Interventions on the Microbiota (pp. 1-23). Elsevier.

Wood, A. M., et al. (2019). Gratitude and well-being: A review and theoretical integration. Clinical Psychology Review, 30(7), 890-905.

www.ingramcontent.com/pod-product-compliance
Lightning Source LLC
Chambersburg PA
CBHW071733120626
46550CB00002B/504